RULE AND TESTAMENT OF ST. FRANCIS

RULE AND TESTAMENT OF ST. FRANCIS

Conferences to the Modern Followers of Francis

By
Cajetan Esser O.F.M.

Rule and Testament of St. Francis: Conferences to the Modern Followers of Francis, by Cajetan Esser O.F.M. Copyright © 1977 by Franciscan Herald Press, 1434 West 51st Street, Chicago, Illinois 60609.

Library of Congress Cataloging in Publication Data:

Esser, Kajetan, 1913-
    Rule and Testament of St. Francis.

    1. Francesco d'Assisi, Saint, 1182-1226. Regula non bullata. 2. Francesco d'Assisi, Saint, 1182-1226. Testamentum. I. Title.
BX3604.Z5E835   255'.3'06   77-5318
ISBN 0-8199-0674-3

NIHIL OBSTAT:
    Mark P. Hegener O.F.M.
    Censor Deputatus

IMPRIMATUR:
    Msgr. Richard A. Rosemeyer, J.C.D.
    Vicar General, Archdiocese of Chicago

July 11, 1977

MADE IN THE UNITED STATES OF AMERICA

Foreword

Fr. Esser's commentary on the Rule of the Order of Friars Minor was presented over a period of several months in 1965 to Franciscan and Capuchin confreres in Germany. The original German lectures, with notes added afterwards by Fr. Esser, were published the same year by Dietrich-Coelde Verlag, Werl, Westphalia, Germany, "pro manuscripto." An English version, based in part on a translation made by Fr. Bruce Malina O.F.M., was published serially in mimeographed form in *Round Table* and then the series was duplicated in brochure form by the Conventual Franciscan Friars of Our Lady of Consolation Province. Although Fr. Esser's learned work, *Origins of the Franciscan Order,* has already appeared in an English version (Franciscan Herald Press, 1970), his previous commentary on the Rule (1965) is of a more direct and simpler nature and well suited for spiritual reading and instruction.

The conferences of Fr. Esser on the Testament of St. Francis, which we have added, are here published for the first time in any language. Fr. Esser gave these conferences in German to the Franciscan Sisters, Daughters of the Sacred Hearts of Jesus and Mary, at their Generalate in Rome (Via della Maglianella, 135) during the period from June, 1974, to March, 1976. They were translated into English by Sister Audrey Marie Rothweil O.S.F. and made available to her fellow Sisters in mimeographed form. Each of the conferences is now presented as a separate chapter of Fr. Esser's commentary on the Testament. Like his reflections on the Rule, these talks on the Testament will prove helpful spiritually to all the followers of the Poverello. — THE EDITOR

CONTENTS

APPENDIX

Part I
THE RULE

I

THE RULE TODAY

Through the Second Vatican Council, the Catholic Church has begun to undergo a thorough overhauling. Her responsible leaders, as they themselves have often attested, are clear on one point — the Church must today cast off the useless ballast with which she has cluttered herself in her course through the centuries if she is to adjust to the needs of the present. And in the deliberations of the Council, it becomes increasingly clearer that such an updating indispensably presupposes an awareness of the Church's origins. Hence in the Council's deliberations, the re-thinking of the Sacred Scriptures holds first rank. The Church is striving, in downright earnest, to live from the Word of God, and from it to forge its way through the present to the future.

The religious orders of the Church have likewise come a long way through history. And on their way, they too have taken much dead freight, which today encumbers and often hinders them from appropriately fulfilling the tasks which the Church expects of them, precisely today. They have to do for themselves in particular, what the Church is trying to do in the Council for the Catholic community in general. Recent Pontiffs have specifically asked the religious orders of the Church to get on with the task of updating — beginning with the directives of Pius XII to the Congress of Religious in 1950[1] to the almost pleaful entreaty of Paul VI to the General Chapters of various Orders in 1964.[2] The Popes always ask for an awareness and a re-thinking of the origins of the respective Orders, so that from the spirit, force, and power of those beginnings an updating to today's tasks and circumstances might be effected.

Like the Church today, religious Orders cannot afford to settle down all too comfortably in their traditions. Certainly no Order is a perfectly built house designed for all ages, in which every piece of furniture has its unchangeable place, so that all the changes in it from generation to generation are its inhabitants. Like the Church, her Orders too are entities alive and living in history, entities which now and again must adjust to concrete circumstances if they do not wish to function as museums, valuable for historical knowledge, but useless for present day needs. For the Church as well as for religious Orders, authentic change from the past to the future is an obligatory task laid upon them by the Lord of History.

This task is equally incumbent upon the Order of Friars Minor. To discharge it is particularly difficult because the Order of St. Francis has coursed through a history marked with lengthy tragic intervals. For the Church of the Middle Ages, the beginnings of the Franciscan Order were so unspeakably new that it was quite difficult, as the Order was then conceived, to fit it into the life of the Church of that day.[3] In many respects, it seems as though the specific hour of the Order has just come today. Therefore the task of re-thinking its beginnings with a view to modern application should be particularly relieving and exhilarating.

The purpose of the study published here is to serve this concern which is so important for the Church and the Order of Friars Minor in the Church. It was presented during the past few months to confreres from the Franciscan and Capuchin Orders. At the insistence of these confreres, it is now presented to a wider audience within the Franciscan Order. For this reason it is published only as manuscript (in German, in 1965).

Here let me admit from the start that this is being done with some hesitation. The author would have preferred to publish these ideas as part of a thorough study of the Rule of the Order, on which he has already labored for many years.[4] On the other hand, he has already been able to publish many works preparatory to the planned full study so that these will justify the present publication. While this paper is printed as it was delivered, many notes have been added to it. These notes refer chiefly to these preparatory studies; they establish the correctness of the analysis of the Rule and the detailed consequences here presented. The reader therefore is asked to round off the judgment he forms while reading this paper by a careful perusal of the references. For only then will he see, point by point, that he must not understand the Rule from the viewpoint of later developments; but that he can arrive at an historically complete understanding of the Rule only through accurate knowledge of the early history of the Order.

Lastly, but not least, the material which up till now has resulted from scientific research and is here presented in a short survey should prove of practical service to the responsible leaders of the Order in the fulfillment of that great task which Pope Paul VI has set before them,[5] and which the supreme moderator of the Order has made so entirely his own.[6] In line with the words of the Pope, our Minister General wishes to effect a *"renovatio disciplinae"* for the Order. With this the Order's supreme authority consciously places itself into one of the most important life-movements of the Church of our time, while at the same time wanting to fulfill those demands of the Father of our Order, who would always have his Friars Minor follow the venerable footsteps of Mother Church with particular devotedness.[7] Hence this contribution of ours is made with the aim of helping fulfill the wish of the supreme authority of the Order: "that the time-honored character of the Order will shine forth, since proper renewal ought to be achieved in such a way that the distinctive character and traditional spirit of the Order remain intact."[8]

NOTES

1. Pius XII, "Allocution to the First Congress of Delegates of Religious Orders, Congregations, Societies and Secular Institutes (Dec. 8, 1950)," *AAS* 43 (1951) 26-36. Cf. Rohrbasser, *Heilslehre der Kirche,* Freiburg/ Schweiz 1953, n. 1443 and 1453.

2. Paul VI, "Allocutio ad summos Moderatores quarundam Familiarum Religiosarum earumque sodales, qui Romam convenerunt ad sui cuiusque Instituti Capitulum Generale (May 23, 1964)," *AAS* 56 (1964) 565-571; cited here and in the following from the *ACTA OFM* 83 (1964), 534-537. — The Pope expressly emphasizes that he considers his statements important for all religious in the whole world (*ibid.,* 534b). In various passages he emphatically points out that this renewal must follow from the given special character of the Order and from the spirit of its founder (*ibid.,* 536b).

3. Cf. the third stanza of the ancient Sequence for the feast of St. Francis, ascribed to Thomas of Celano: "Novus ordo, nova vita — Mundo surgit inaudita," (*AnalFranc* X, 402). For a thorough treatment of the problem here indicated, cf. K. Esser O.F.M., "Gestald und Ideal des Minderbrüderordens in seinen Anfängen," in *FranzStud* 39 (1957) 1-22.

4. Fr. Esser's *Origins of the Franciscan Order,* translated by A. Daly and I. Lynch, 289 pp., was published by Franciscan Herald Press in 1970.

5. "This renewal of discipline also demands that it proceed only by way of competent authority," Paul VI, "Allocutio," *art. cit.,* 536b.

6. Augustinus Sépinski O.F.M., *Litterae Ministri Generalis de Ordine Fratrum Minorum ad hodiernas condiciones accommodando,* Feb. 22, 1965.

7. 2 Celano 24.

8. Sépinski, *op. cit.,* 7f.

II

PRELIMINARY CONSIDERATIONS

Three basic factors, lodged in the past history of our Order, render our present-day understanding of the Rule more difficult and even promote in us a certain uneasy feeling towards the Rule itself. These are: the influence of legend, which in any given situation often proves an obstacle to the attainment of historical truth; the influence of asceticism, which is quick to give a "pious" interpretation to everything; and the influence of law, often in the form of a frightening legalism, which had especially baneful repercussions in the area under consideration. All three factors bear a heavy weight of guilt for the fact that we are not entirely content with the Rule of our Order and feel a certain revulsion at the mention of "regular observance." These three considerations often make it difficult for us to give whole-hearted expression to that promise which, at our profession, we minister, to the Church on earth, that promise "to observe all the days of my life the Rule of the Friars Minor." At the outset of our considerations, then, let us focus further attention on these three points.

The Influence of Legend

To this stubborn and well-nigh unshakeable domain belong

views such as the following. The present Rule of our Order was imposed upon St. Francis, contrary to his innermost convictions, by the Roman Curia, because the Curia wished to fit the young Order into the framework of its political designs; Francis did in fact bend to the will of the Church in heroic faith; but towards the end of his life, as maintained especially by P. Sabatier, he lashed out in his Testament with a searing condemnation of this tyranny.[1] A second version of this legend would claim that the text of the Rule as written by Francis was watered down by a faction composed of the ministers and scholars of the Order; the Rule appeared too strict for these men and, consequently, they proceeded to strike out from their own text a number of core-ideas central to original Franciscan idealism. What remained was at best a compromise position which really satisfied no one, and thus laid the groundwork for many subsequent disputes in the Order.[2] Mild, by way of contrast, is the less dramatic view that Francis found himself compelled to tone down his idealism in the Rule in order to accommodate his Rule to the demands of an Order which in the meantime had grown to worldwide propor-tions. In one case he went too far; in the other case, not far enough.[3] The underlying conclusion to all these approaches, how-ever, which seem to form the dramatic highpoint of almost every Franciscan biography,[4] is that in consequence we can make our commitment to the Rule as it now stands only with the greatest difficulty!

The Influence of Asceticism

In the process of the Order's adaptation to the monastic form of life, which apparently was deemed indispensably necessary in the thirteenth century by the men of the Middle Ages, an inter-pretation of the Rule gained prominence which I would like to term the "ascetic" view. It, too, in turn, had its undesirable effects on the understanding of the original sense of the Rule. This fact might be verified by almost countless examples, but here a few instances from the *Speculum Perfectionis*[5] will suffice to illus-trate the point.

According to the fifth chapter of the Rule, the friars worked solely and simply to provide themselves with the necessary means of livelihood; according to the *Speculum Perfectionis* (27, 11), they worked in order to mortify their bodies. The Rule, in the sixth chapter, exhorts the friars to look after the needs of their brothers with the loving care of a mother; the *Speculum Perfectionis,* on the other hand, has Francis say, after he had been moved by spontaneous love to help a brother in need: "Dearest brothers, necessity and charity for my brother have moved me to act as I have done. . . . But I do not wish to do so again, for it would be neither regular nor fitting for friars to do so (27, 10). Here, then, the religious "decorum" of the friar has become more important than the love prescribed in the rule! — The Rule allows the friars in a "manifest necessity" to journey on horseback; the *Speculum Perfectionis* restricts this to a "most pressing need" (35, 7).

This ascetic approach is made crystal clear in the so-called "Testament of the Blessed Francis for the Portiuncula" from which the *Speculum Perfectionis* is eager to quote.[6] According to this "Testament," only those clerics ought to live at the Portiuncula who have been chosen from among the finest and holiest friars of the whole Order and who pray the Office especially well "so that both layfolk and the other friars may see and hear them gladly and with great devotion." Holy and humble lay-brothers should be assigned in order to "serve them" (55, 33-34). Even prescinding from the fact that the ascetic goals set forth here are totally at odds with Francis' spiritual vision, the life of these friars is presented in the context of a monastic form of life that was foreign to the early days of the Order.

Here we see, then, that simple daily occurrences in the life of Francis take on ascetical significance and are transformed into "means of perfection" which ironically, on the one hand, even dispense with the obligations of fraternal charity while, on the other hand, reveal that class distinction in the fraternity which weighs down so heavily on the Order even to this day. From such a point of view it is not far to that mentality which main-

tains that whoever has made a vow of poverty is dispensed from
the obligation of almsgiving. This was a view which Francis
repeatedly overrode with unqualified scorn to the obvious dis-
comfort of later ascetical writers!

The Influence of Legalistic Mentality

The influence of a legalistic mentality has had the most disastrous consequences of all. Our Rule took shape at a time when
jurisprudence began to flourish and casuistry was paving its
way to a position of importance. Hence it took only a short time
(and, if we think of the Bull *"Quo elongati"* of 1230, it was a
matter of only a few years) for the Rule to become a *legal document.* Juridical methods of interpretation were then applied to
establish the exact legal meaning and legal obligation of the
Rule.[7] Perhaps Francis sought to fend off this development already
in his Testament (n. 12).[8] Be that as it may, his efforts were without success. For, despite his urgent admonition, the thirteenth
century already witnessed expositions of the Rule which aimed
primarily at establishing those obligations to which the friars
were bound (and, especially to which they were *not* bound) "in
virtue of the vow" and "in virtue of a precept." This development
reached its initial climax in an anonymous exposition of the Rule,
dating from the 13th/14th century, which drew out a total of
61 (!) gravely binding precepts from the text of the Rule.[9] Against
this type of unhealthy exaggeration, the Popes later determined
that there are only 25 gravely binding precepts (*vota et praecepta*),[10] which became the basic framework of every exposition of
the Rule in the Order. Yet we must all admit that these explanations of the Rule with their detailed casuistry, even when published under the title of the "Book of Life"[11] have never awakened
any enthusiasm for regular observance in us, with the possible
exception of those eager to discover therein vindication for a
particularly strict Order.

These juridical expositions naturally bypassed all those declarations in the Rule which were considered "merely" admonitions,
for such exhortations simply do not lend themselves to juridical

treatment in the strict sense. Yet, as will be evident, it is precisely these exhortations which express most profoundly what St. Francis himself desired. The question, therefore, already arises: What sort of wording did Francis himself consider indicative of the greater obligation: to begin a sentence with "I firmly command," "I prescribe under obedience," and the like; or to begin with "I counsel, admonish, and exhort my brothers in our Lord Jesus Christ?" In the latter, Francis so to say conceals his own person "in our Lord Jesus Christ" in order to proclaim the marrow of the Gospel in Christ's own words. This is precisely the insight which these "expositions of the Rule" have almost entirely neglected due to the nature of their juridical aims.

For this reason these expositions of the Rule must perhaps bear the main burden of guilt for the fact that today, in all three branches of the Order of Friars Minor, voices are being raised calling for a new Rule for the First Order of St. Francis. After all, so the argument runs, Leo XIII gave the Third Order Secular a new Rule adapted to modern conditions, and Pius XI did the same for the Third Order Regular. Behind this wish, however, lies a persuasion — even if not explicitly formulated in so many words — that the Rule has lost contact with real life due to centuries of casuistry and the legal fictions which such casuistry spawned, and that the Rule has become so juridically orientated that it can no longer be brought into harmony with the existential life of the Order. And there, in a word, lies our specific problem!

An Age-old Problem

The problem as thus outlined, of course, is certainly not of recent vintage. Its roots lie deep in the history of the Order. By way of example, we need only turn to the famous first chapter of the *Speculum Perfectionis.*[12]

The contents of the chapter are well-known. Francis, wishing to compose a definitive Rule for his friars, went up the mountain at Fonte Colombo. The ministers, with a somewhat reluctant Brother Elias in tow, came to Francis to prevent him from drawing up too harsh a Rule. After an appropriate prayer on the part of

Francis, the voice of Christ was heard to ring out: "Francis, nothing in this Rule is yours; for all is Mine. I wish the Rule to be obeyed to the letter, to the letter, without gloss, without gloss."

This account betrays layers of legend, and its stages of development may be traced rather exactly. The essential kernel was no doubt occasioned by the disagreements attending the mendicant disputes of the second half of the thirteenth century. These discussions revolved around the Gospel character of the life of the Friars Minor and its integration into the life of the Church.[13] In its more particularized present-day formulation, the problem dates back to the Order's debate with John XXII over the traditional poverty of the Order. This dispute, as is well-known, led to a schism between the Order and the Church. But if the content of the Rule, as maintained in the *Speculum Perfectionis,* stems entirely from Christ and was, so to say, personally dictated by Christ Himself, then evidently Christ's Vicar on earth can neither condemn the Order's concept of poverty as set forth in the Rule nor declare it to be an ideal beyond realization. Along with this historically conditioned circumstance, this account reveals a second factor at work. From the lips of Christ Himself and repeatedly at that — in opposition to His own Vicar on earth, and in opposition to all casuists as well — comes a condemnation of every juridical exposition of the Rule. The double "to the letter" and the triple "without gloss" demanded by Christ Himself were destined to shape the future centuries. The legendary voice of Fonte Colombo became a powerful determinant in the history of the Order.

A further insight reveals that the account aims at portraying Francis as a new Moses receiving the law of the Lord on a new Sinai and thereby encountering opposition from the new People of God. But, as so often happens in similar cases, here legend begins development. It had made Francis, like Moses, a lawgiver in virtue of a divine commission.[14] Accordingly, his law, i.e. his Rule, has also become sacrosanct. Small wonder, then, that the Rule suffered the same fate as the Mosaic Law in the late Judaic Talmud. Law was no longer at the service of life, but life was at the service of law. Within this perspective the account of the *Speculum Perfectionis,* often retold, even more often reprinted and, to top it all off, even supported by a vision of St. Bridget,[15] has perpetuated its particular problems down to the present day. At the very outset of his study of the exposition of the Rule, the novice is still confronted with the question: "What does it mean to observe the Rule of the Friars Minor *to the letter?"*[16]

This question merits two observations from the historian. First, the phrase "to the letter" must always be seen from its juridical point of view and, consequently, in the context of the legalistic mentality of its day and not in reference to the genuine text of the Rule. Secondly, without doubt an interesting study could be written on the subject of how often Francis himself acted contrary to the letter of his Rule[17] because, as both Celano and Bonaventure agree, "he placed the Gospel above all other prescriptions."[18] I am personally convinced that Francis himself was never conscious of standing in a legislator-law relationship to his Rule, as the jurists claim.

In any case, it must be granted — in the light of our thesis — that the legend of a Rule dictated by Christ Himself has hindered and continues to hinder us from understanding the Rule in its historical evolution; from considering it once and for all as an historical document and not as a juridical document, i.e. of inquiring into the "Sitz im Leben" of the individual statements of the Rule. Only when this inquiry has yielded its answers, can we posit the further question, namely, what meaning can these statements have for us today?[19] Our reflections on the subject will hopefully serve this goal.

NOTES

1. Cf. K. Esser, *Das Testament des hl. Franziskus von Assisi. Eine Untersuchung über seine Echtheit und seine Bedeutung.* Münster i.W. 1949, 5f — In order not to overburden the footnotes unduly, the citations of the standard works and periodicals will follow those abbreviations as listed in the collection *Franziskanische Quellenschriften.* English translations of the primary sources will be found in the *Omnibus of Sources* published by

Franciscan Herald Press in 1973 — third revised edition in 1977.

2. *Speculum Perfectionis* (ed. Sabatier-Little, Manchester 1928), chap. 3 and parallels! This version of the *Speculum Perfectionis* arose about 1328 in the territory of the Cologne Province of the Friars Minor; cf. Esser, *Das Testament*, 34f.

3. Angelus Clarenus, *Expositio regulae fratrum minorum* (ed. Oliger, Quaracchi 1912) 204f. — We should note here that contrary to their modern successors, the poverty zealots of the 14th century held the definitive Rule of the Order in the highest regard. Its authority was never questioned.

4. This "drama" which never took place has already been critically discussed by Fidentius van den Borne, "Het 'drama' in de moderne Franciscusbiografie," in *Sint Franciscus* 2 (1956) 248-287.

5. Ed. Little-Sabatier, chap. 1.

6. Concerning this "Testament" of St. Francis, which is a typical example of the formation of legend, all that is pertinent can be found in Esser, *Das Testament*, 14-16.

7. H. Grundmann, "Die Bulle 'Quo elongati' Papst Gregors IX," in *ArchFranchHist* 54 (1961) 3ff.

8. Cf. Esser, *Das Testament*, 196ff.

9. "Expositio super regulam Fratrum Minorum edita a quibusdam ordinis," in *Speculum Minorum*, Venice 1513, pars III, fol. 68rb-70rb.

10. Isidorus Trienekens O.F.M., *Vota et praecepta regulae fratrum minorum*, Quaracchi 1909.

11. Kilian Kazenberger O.F.M., *Liber vitae seu Regulae s. Francisci expositio*, Quaracchi 1926.

12. Ed. Little-Sabatier 1, 1-8. — The account is to be found, though in widely divergent forms, in nearly all 14th century documents dealing with Francis' life. Surprisingly, it is lacking in those of the 13th century. Regarding the so-called "Verba sancti patris Francisci," ascribed to Bro. Leo (d. 1271), there are grave doubts concerning not only its authenticity but its veracity as well.

13. Cf. Bonaventure, "Sermo V de s. p. n. Francisco," (Op. Omnia, IX, 590ff.), where in n. 10 the rule is still presented as originating from a "divine revelation" in close agreement with the *Testamentum s. Francisci* (n. 12; *Opuscula* 82; *Analekten* 39). — The formation of legend would certainly have seized upon this for support.

14. Sophronius Clasen O.F.M., "Franziskus, der neue Moses," in *Wiss-Weish* 24 (1961) 202ff.

15. Cf. Kazenberger, *Liber vitae*, 4.

16. *Ibid.*, 5ff. — Opposed to such an approach today is the exhortation of the Pope to religious: "But if it should happen that the *letter* of your Rules will in fact change, the *spirit* of your Rules will remain intact." Paul VI, "Allocutio ad summos Moderatores," *art. cit.*, 536b. It could not have been put more clearly!

17. Cf. Sophronius Clasen O.F.M., "Die Armut als Beruf: Franziskus von Assisi," in *Miscellanea Mediaevalia* 3, Berlin 1964, 78.

18. "Placing the holy Gospel before all otther institutions"; 2 Celano 216; *Legenda maior* XIV, 5. In those days, "institutions" meant those monastic prescriptions which are called "statutes" today. This clarification gives the words of the biographers far reaching significance.

19. The *Werkbuch zur Regel des hl. Franziskus,* Werl i. W. 1955 was too little attentive to this "Sitz im Leben." (Eng. trans., *The Marrow of the Gospel,* Franciscan Herald Press, Chicago, 1968).

III

PRELIMINARY NOTES

Before going into an historical analysis of the text of the Rule, a few important preliminary remarks are in order.

1. From the manuscript tradition of all the *Opuscula* of St. Francis, we discover a great variation in the headings affixed to individual chapters as well as in the form and content of these chapters. This is borne out especially in the manuscript tradition of the *"Regula non bullata,"* for which we even have one textual witness with no headings at all.[1] As is still evident today from his Testament, Francis dictated his Admonitions and Letters without headings for supposedly individual chapters. As our analysis will clearly indicate, we may conclude that this holds true also for the first written copy of the Rule. Our present-day division of the Rule into chapters is not contained in the original; in fact, this division tends to separate important connected ideas and often enough does not indicate the precise relationship of one idea with those which follow. This is most evident in the present chapters 2, 6, 10, 11, and 12 of the Rule,[2] where the headings represent at best a questionable "part for the whole." At any rate, however, these headings were already contained in the papal Bull of Confirmation and, consequently, would have been added

to some extent though very superficially to the Rule even before
the papal confirmation. The reason for this is to be found in the
fact that at that time a Rule, if only for its liturgical usage, needed
some kind of division into chapters. For in those days, and as is
still the case among the older Orders, a section of the Rule of the
Order was read as the "lectio brevis" at the "conclusion of the
Chapter" at the end of Prime.

For an analysis of the text of the Rule, therefore, it is best
to leave the headings with their chapter divisions conveniently
aside. Had this been observed in the past, a number of misinter-
pretations of the Rule may have been avoided. We need only recall the inner continuity of our present Chapters 5 and 6 of the
Rule. A realization of their intimate connection would have made
many a dispute over the relationship between work and asking
alms a superfluous discussion.

Hence we must bid farewell to that age-old mentality which
would have us see in the twelve chapters of the Rule a symbol
of an "apostolic Rule." According to this view, Francis would
have divided the Rule into twelve chapters because he wanted
to indicate that the Rule was established on the twelve apostolic
foundation stones, and that the Rule symbolized the twelve gates
through which we enter into the "Gospel life" as into the new
Jerusalem which comes down from God and on whose twelve
gates are inscribed the names of the twelve Apostles.[3] The historical truth is certainly more sober, and stands in no need of
such mystical flights of fancy.

2. Francis did not think logically, in our sense of the word,
but in terms of concrete association.[4] This is particularly evident
in his Testament, but also in his other writings. Now it is clear,
however, from an impartial reading of the Rule, that whatever
inner logic is contained in it has been destroyed in its present
arrangement. The chapters often combine unrelated subjects; the
transitions from one chapter to another follow no logical sequence.
For example, take the theme of the "activity of the friars" chapters
5 and 9 of the Rule, where it appears to be treated respectively
with a surprising continuity or — to our way of thinking — a

surprising lack of continuity. Though in retrospect the influence of legend makes this somewhat understandable, it is actually hard to comprehend why up until now the question of the Rule's inner structure, i.e. especially in terms of its inner principle of arrangement, has never been posed. The problem might be put thus: Why do the directives of the Rule follow in their present order and not in some other order? Or to put the problem in different words: "What did Francis want to 'regulate' when he wrote his 'regula'?" This question provides the real key to an analysis on the text of the Rule without the traditional headings but arranged rather in meaningful sentences established from the text itself.

IV

TEXT OF THE RULE

In the Name of the Lord!
Here Begins the Life of the Friars Minor

1. This is the Rule and Life of the Friars Minor, namely, to observe the Holy Gospel of our Lord Jesus Christ, living in obedience, without property, and in chastity.
2. Brother Francis promises obedience and reverence to our Lord Pope Honorius and his successors canonically elected, and to the Roman Church: and the other brothers are bound to obey Brother Francis and his successors.
3. If anyone wish to adopt this life and come to our friars, let them send him to the Minister Provincial, to whom alone, and to no other is granted leave to receive the friars.
4. And the Minister shall examine him carefully concerning the Catholic Faith and the Sacraments of the Church. And if he believe in all these things and will faithfully profess and steadfastly observe them to the end; and if he have no wife, or if having one, she has already entered a convent or has given him permission by authority of the bishop of the diocese, — she herself, having previously made a vow of con-

tinence and being such age that no suspicion can be raised against her — then the Minister shall address to him the words of the Holy Gospel — that he go and sell all that he has and take care to give it to the poor; but if he cannot do this his good will shall suffice.

5. And the friars and the Minister shall take heed not to be solicitous about his temporal goods, so that he may dispose of his property freely as the Lord shall inspire him.

6. If, however, counsel be sought, the Minister may send him to some God-fearing persons according to whose advice his goods shall be distributed to the poor.

7. Then shall be given him the clothes of probation, namely, two tunics without the hood, and the cord, and drawers, and the *caperone* reaching to the cord, unless it should seem good to the same Minister, before God, to act otherwise.

8. The year of his probation being finished, let him be received to obedience, promising to observe always this Rule and Life.

9. And on no account shall it be lawful for him to leave this Order, as decreed by our Lord the Pope, for, according to the Holy Gospel, no man putting his hand to the plow and looking back is fit for the Kingdom of God.

10. Let those who have already promised obedience have one tunic with a hood, and another (if they wish) without the hood. And those who are compelled by necessity may wear shoes. And all the friars shall wear coarse garments, and they may mend them with sacking and other pieces of cloth, with the blessing of God.

11. And I admonish and exhort them not to despise nor judge those whom they see dressed in soft and fine clothes and who use dainty food and drink; but rather let everyone judge and despise himself.

12. The clerics shall recite the divine office according to the use of the Roman Church, excepting the psalter; for which reason they may have breviaries. But the lay-brethren shall say twenty-four Our Fathers for Matins, and five for Lauds;

seven for each of the Hours of Prime, Tierce, Sext, and None; twelve for Vespers, and seven for Compline; they shall also pray for the dead.

13. And the friars shall fast from the feast of All Saints until Christmas. But with regard to the Lent which begins at the Epiphany and lasts during the forty days which our Lord consecrated by His own fast, let those who keep it voluntarily be blessed by the Lord; but those who do not wish to keep it shall not be obliged. But they shall fast during the other Lent which lasts until our Lord's Resurrection. At other times they shall not be bound to fast except on Fridays. In cases, however, of manifest necessity, the friars are not obliged to observe corporal fasts.

14. I counsel, admonish, and exhort my brethren in Jesus Christ that when they go out in the world they neither quarrel nor dispute nor judge others; but let them be meek, peaceful, modest, gentle, and humble; speaking courteously to everyone, as is becoming.

15. They shall not ride unless compelled by manifest necessity, or by infirmity.

16. Into whatever house they enter they shall first say: Peace be to this house.

17. And according to the Holy Gospel they may partake of whatever food is set before them.

18. I strictly command all the friars that they by no means receive coin or money, either by themselves or through the medium of others.

19. Nevertheless, the Ministers and Custodes, and they only, shall take special care to provide for the needs of the sick and the clothing of the other friars, through their spiritual friends, according to places, seasons, and cold climates, as they may deem necessary; saving always that, as before said, they receive neither coin nor money.

20. Those friars whom the Lord has given the grace of working, shall work faithfully and devotedly, in such wise that avoiding idleness, the enemy of the soul, they yet do not extinguish

the spirit of holy prayer and devotion to which all temporal things ought to be subservient.

21a. In payment for their work let them receive whatever is necessary for the bodily support of themselves and their brethren; excepting coin or money. And this they should do humbly as becomes the servants of God and followers of most holy poverty.

21b. The friars shall appropriate to themselves nothing, neither house nor place nor anything at all.

22. But as pilgrims and strangers in this world, serving the Lord in poverty and humility, they shall go seeking alms with confidence. Nor ought they to be ashamed, since for our sakes our Lord made Himself poor in this world.

23. This is that sublime height of most exalted poverty which has made you, my most beloved brethren, heirs and kings of the Kingdom of Heaven; which has made you poor in temporal things but exalted you in virtue. Let this be your portion which leads into the Land of the Living. Giving yourselves up wholly to this, beloved brethren, never seek anything else under heaven for the sake of our Lord Jesus Christ.

24. And wherever any of the friars may be and shall meet other friars, let them all treat each other as members of one family, and confidently make known to each other their needs; for if a mother loves and cherishes her son according to the flesh, how much more diligently ought everyone to cherish and love him who is his brother according to the spirit.

25. And when any friar falls sick,[5] the other friars shall serve him as they would wish to be served themselves.

26. If any friar, at the instigation of the enemy, sin mortally in regard to any of those sins concerning which it has been ordained among the brethren to have recourse only to the Ministers Provincial, let him have recourse as quickly as possible and without delay. And, if the said Ministers are priests, they shall with mercy impose on him a penance; but, if the Ministers are not priests, they shall cause it to be

imposed by others who are priests of the Order, as in the sight of God shall appear to them more expedient.

27. And they shall take care not to get angry or disturbed by the sins of others, for anger and trouble of spirit are hindrances to charity in themselves and in others.

28. All the friars are bound to have always one of the friars of this Order as Minister General and servant of the whole Fraternity, and they shall be strictly obliged to obey him.

29. When he dies, his successor shall be elected by the Ministers Provincial and the Custodes in the Chapter of Pentecost. At this Chapter all the Ministers Provincial shall assemble in whatever place the Minister General shall appoint.

30. This they shall do once in every three years, or at other periods, longer or shorter, as the aforesaid Minister shall ordain. And if at any time it should appear to the body of the Ministers Provincial and Custodes that the aforesaid Minister General is not qualified for the service and general welfare of the friars, the aforesaid friars to whom the election is committed shall be bound to elect another as Custos in the name of the Lord.

31. Moreover, after the Chapter of Pentecost, the Ministers Provincial and Custodes may each, if they wish, and deem it expedient, convoke a Chapter of the friars in their custodies once in the same year.

32. The friars shall not preach in the diocese of any bishop, when the latter has opposed their doing so. And no friar shall by any means dare to preach to the people, unless he has been examined and approved by the Minister General of this Fraternity, and the office of preacher has been conferred upon him.

33. Moreover, I admonish and exhort these same friars that when they preach, their language be well-considered and simple, for the benefit and edification of the people, discoursing to them of vices and virtues, punishment and glory, with brevity, because our Lord when on earth made "a short word."

34. Those friars who are the Ministers and servants of the others

shall visit and admonish their brethren, and humbly and charitably correct them; not commanding them anything that is against their own soul and our Rule.

35. But the brethren, who are subjects, shall remember that, for God's sake, they have renounced their own wills. Wherefore, I strictly command them to obey their Ministers in all things they have promised the Lord to observe, and which are not against their soul or our Rule.

36. And wherever those friars may be who know and feel that they cannot observe the Rule spiritually, they can and should have recourse to their Ministers. And the Ministers should receive them charitably and kindly and show such familiarity that these same friars may speak and treat with them as masters with their servants; for so it ought to be that the Ministers should be the servants of all the friars.

37a. I also admonish and exhort the friars in our Lord Jesus Christ to beware of all pride, vainglory, envy, and avarice, of care and solicitude for the things of this world, of detraction and murmuring. And those who are illiterate shall not be anxious to learn.

37b. But let them endeavor to have, what is to be above all things desired, the Spirit of the Lord, and His holy operation: let them endeavor to pray always with a pure heart, and to have humility and patience in persecution and infirmity, and to love those who persecute, reprove and censure us, because our Lord says: "Love your enemies and pray for those who persecute and calumniate you. Blessed are they who suffer persecution for justice sake, since theirs is the Kingdom of Heaven. He who perseveres to the end, he shall be saved.

38a. I strictly command all the friars not to have any suspicious dealings or conversation with women.

38b. Nor shall they enter the convents of nuns, excepting those friars to whom special leave is granted by the Apostolic See.

38c. Neither shall they be godfathers to men or women,[6] lest hereby scandal should arise either among the friars or concerning them.

39. Should any friars moved by divine inspiration desire to go among the Saracens or other infidels, they shall ask leave to go from their Ministers Provincial. But the Ministers shall not grant leave except to those whom they deem fit to be sent.

40. Finally I command the Ministers by obedience that they petition our Lord the Pope for one of the Cardinals of the Holy Roman Church, who shall be the governor, protector, and corrector of this Fraternity; so that, being always submissive and subject at the feet of the same Holy Church, and steadfast in the Catholic Faith, we may observe poverty and humility and the Holy Gospel of our Lord Jesus Christ, as we have firmly promised.

NOTES

1. Cod. Q 27 of the Cathedral Library of Worcester; cf. Esser, "Zur Textgeschichte der Regula non bullata des hl. Franziskus," in *FranzStud* 33 (1951) 219ff.

2. Cf. the critical edition of (L. Lemmens O.F.M.) *Opuscula sancti Patris Francisci Assisiensis,* Quaracchi 1904, 63-74; H. Boehmer, *Analekten zur Geschichte des Franciscus von Assisi,* Tübingen 1904, 29-35. — Both scholars used the still extant original Bull with the text of the Rule; yet both allow themselves the liberty to correct this text, as will be pointed out later. These editions will henceforth be cited as: *Opuscula . . . ; Analekten . . . .*

3. Cf. Ub. de Casali, *Arbor vitae crucifixae Jesu,* Venice 1485, lib. V, col. V, Ejjj.

4. Cf. Esser, *Das Testament,* 125ff; for the *Exhortations* and the *Letters to All Christians,* cf. Boehmer, *Analekten* XLI, note 1.

5. The original Bull, as Lemmens, *Opuscula* 169, has rightly noted, has "in infirmitate!" Yet both editors changed it to "in infirmitatem." All the manuscripts of the *Regula non bullata* (chap. 10) also give as the text: "Si quis fratrum *in infirmitate* ceciderit," contrary to the unfounded reading of both critical editions. Therefore, we will keep to *"in infirmitate"* and interpret the phrase according to the sense of this reading.

6. What was noted in no. 24 above also applies here. The critical editions replace the correlative *"nec........nec"* of the original Bull (*"neither* shall they be godfathers to men or women *nor* let scandal arise in this regard . . .")* with *"nec........ne"* (*"neither* shall they be godfathers to men or women, *lest* thereby scandal should arise . . .")* to infer a logical consequence. Cf. *Werkbuch zur Regel,* 251f (English trans., cf. footnote 19, chapter II).

V

ANALYSIS OF THE TEXT

"Here begins the Life of the Friars Minor"[1] is, so to say, the title of the Rule that follows. This title itself is most informative. In line with medieval usage, we might have expected: "Here begins the *Rule* of the Friars Minor." But instead the title reads *"Life"* — a decisively key word for the understanding of the Rule. The Rule is intended to be a presentation, description and regulation of a particular way of life. According to its meaning then, we should translate the title: "Here begins a description of the way of life of the Friars Minor." For, as will be pointed out, Francis does in fact describe in the Rule the manner of living of the friars of his day, as it had developed up to 1223;[2] in the Rule, the founder indicates how they, as Friars Minor, are to lead this life of theirs.

The name of the friars, which we meet in the title, calls for a digression.[3] They are not called "poor Catholics," as so many related groups in the medieval religious poverty movement styled themselves. Nor are they called the "poor of Christ," as they were sometimes referred to in the terminology of this movement and as later legend liked to call them. And no longer are they the "poor little ones," as they did in fact call themselves in their early be-

ginnings. Rather they are *minores fratres,* lesser brothers. The main
word, the noun, in this designation is *fratres,* brothers; the adjec-
tive is *minores,* lesser. According to their name, then, their chief
concern is being brothers, a *fraternitas;* being lowly, being poor, a
minoritas, is the added modifier. The *minoritas* is subordinated to
and directed toward the *fraternitas.* Francis himself liked to call
his new Order the *fraternitas,* the brotherhood.[4]

Throughout their history, the friars have time and again wran-
gled, battled and split with each other over poverty, so much so
that today they live in a schism which is no longer intelligible.
In the Middle Ages and after, not a few friars were greatly intent
upon a falsely understood, outward poverty, which today we can
see stemmed more from contemporary Catharism than from the
Rule and attitude of St. Francis.[5] For the sake of this type of
poverty, the friars have gambled away both the *fraternitas* as well
as, and above all, the genuine *minoritas,* the real *"mysterium
paupertatis"* of St. Francis.[6] And in so doing they have become
something of an anomaly both in themselves and in their essential
interest. Fixed concentration upon the Catharistic "material poverty" brought a shift in emphasis to the Order, a shift which almost
entirely submerged the main concern of the new group, namely,
Gospel brotherhood. Undoubtedly the distinctionless name *fratres*
for all the members of the Order, and *fraternitas* for the Order
itself, should have guarded against such a deviation. But were not
these names neatly eliminated from the terminology of the Order,
especially in the redaction of our *Constitutiones generales?* The
terminology of the Rule and that of the Constitutions obviously
contradict each other![7]

As already noted, the concept "life" is most important for the
understanding of the Rule. Francis wrote the Rule for the friars
of his day; and they naturally were fully acquainted with their
own concrete way of life. Thus the Rule presupposes that this
concrete way of life is already fully known to all. We, on the
other hand, must first learn what this "Sitz im Leben" was from
other contemporary sources. Now we today are in the fortunate
position of having sure knowledge of the "life of the Friars Minor"

at the time when the Rule was composed. We can once more answer the question as to what this way of life was in the concrete. And this is imperative, for it was this way of life that Francis wanted to animate with the spirit of *fraternitas* and *minoritas* through his Rule. In this same spirit of *fraternitas* and *minoritas,* it is again possible to view the concrete life of those days in relation to the spiritual intent of the Rule. Consequently, we are now able to give a thoroughly adequate answer to the question: What must be the way of life of the Friars Minor today, if it is to arrive at an authentic incarnation of this spirit in daily living?

That the comprehensive word "life" is used here instead of the then usual "rule" makes it quite apparent that the Rule of the Friars Minor is not intended to be a piece of legislation like the Rules of the monastic Orders, which seek to regulate each and every thing in detail. Our Rule does not belong — and this has been sensed from very early on in the Order — to those Rules "which instruct one how to live in an orderly manner in such and such a way."[8] Rather, our Rule is an attempt to fill a specific, already existing way of life with the right spirit. Thus it is a collection of directives, of commands and prohibitions, of admonitions and warnings, which are always concerned with the *right way of living.*

This gives rise to a difficulty which has plagued the history of the Order since its very beginnings and onward. In numbers the Order developed very quickly and spread in a short time over the whole of Europe and beyond. This phenomenal growth was too fast even for St. Francis. He feared and lamented the great number of friars.[9] Naturally, quite soon the concrete "Life of the Friars Minor" to which the Rule was to impart spirit, was no longer recognizable in the Order itself.[10] If one might thus express it, it may be said that body and spirit had become divorced from one another. As a result, the friars clung to the letter in hopes of saving the spirit. The "observe the Rule spiritually" which St. Francis himself demands in the Rule gradually grew to an exclusive "observe the Rule literally," as Chapter 1 of the *Speculum Perfectionis* shows. The friars were no longer concerned with the relationship

between *life* and spirit, but between *letter* and spirit. The rift
between Life and Rule grew ever greater. And along with this, the
practical day to day life of the Order was soon governed by and
hence developed according to other principles, namely, the laws
requiring an accommodation of the Order to a cloistered, monastic way of life. To be sure, history shows us very clearly that such
an accommodation was indispensably necessary for men of the
Middle Ages.[11] But it cannot be denied that, due to this accommodation, it became most difficult to understand the original sense
of the Rule. The Rule was out of context. And in place of the
Rule came the ever more voluminous General Constitutions, which
in their 36 successive editions[12] simply enlarged upon and "can-
onized" the monastic accommodations of the 13th century. Despite
their literary arrangement according to the 12 chapters of the
Rule, the Constitutions continue to stand in latent antithesis to the
Rule. In the following analysis, therefore, we do well not to interpret the Rule from the viewpoint of the present day Constitutions, but rather to once again take our "Life and Rule" seriously
and in their proper context.

Sentence 1:   Note that Francis' use of the word "rule" is of
the *Regula non ·bullata,* "life" is always used instead of "rule,"
even where there is reference to the Rule *fixed in writing.* For
Francis, both words remain in some way synonymous. Perhaps
it was only gradually that he came to use "rule" with any habitual
frequency. His Testament positively suggests this conjecture. —
Sentence 1 precisely defines the first element, the initial com-
ponent, of the life of the Friars Minor, namely, life "after the
manner of the Holy Gospel," as Francis expresses it in his Testament, n. 4.[14] In the concrete, this means living according to the
evangelical counsels, which Francis always conceived as thoroughly
imbued with the Gospel.[15] Hence the first and decisive element is
that the Friars Minor should live the Gospel. This is their *forma
vitae,* their way of life!

Sentence 2:   Contrary to a number of medieval heretical move-
ments which sought to lead the Gospel life while opposing the
hierarchical sacramental Church, the friars' basic concern is to

have their way of life firmly imbedded in obedience to the Church.[16]
According to the text of the Rule, this obedience is rendered in a
genuine personal-hierarchical fashion — from the friars to the minister general; from the minister general as "head of the Order"[17]
to the Lord Pope and the Church of Rome. With this the "tenor
of our life"[18] is clearly defined. It is "life in conformity with the
holy Gospel" within the context of "life in conformity with the
holy Roman Church." Here is a foundation valid for all times, even
while continually calling for re-evaluation, for on it all else must
be built.

Sentence 3:   Following the basic affirmation of the first two
sentences, Francis turns his attention to reception into the brotherhood. Significantly, there is no mention here of those who want to
enter a monastery, but rather of those who "wish to adopt this
form of life," a constant and characteristic phrase of Francis[19]
because it more fittingly expressed his concept of a "common life"
among the friars rather than the "community life" of a monastery.
— The right to receive new members is here incumbent upon the
ministers provincial, whereas up until then it had belonged to the
saint alone.[20] — It is also of interest that here and in the following sentence, the "ministers provincial" clearly emerge as higher
authorities, as men with a real responsibility. Yet neither here nor
in what follows in the Rule is their office in any way juridically determined. The rule presupposes that all the friars know who the
ministers provincial are and what their office entails.[21] These aspects, accordingly, are not "regulated" in the Rule. Instead, the
ministers are simply given norms relative to how they are to discharge the individual obligations of their office. And with this the
Rule's basic concern already emerges, namely, to antimate an
existing way of life with the right attitude. This is immediately
apparent in the following sentence.

Sentence 4:   Francis expects the ministers provincial to discharge the permission or "leave" granted them in the right spirit.
He sees no need to spell this out in minute detail. Francis simply
wants to insure that in the reception of the new friars — in line
with the "tenor of our life" — everything will be in conformity

with evangelical life as well as in conformity with the Church. Those to be received must be free from heresy, ready to lead a genuinely ecclesial life until death, prepared to give up all family ties and, above all, completely detached from all their possessions.[22] Francis always insisted that only those who were truly "without property" (expropriate) could be received into the brotherhood.[23] In this sentence we also meet with two words which Francis never used in reference to the friars themselves: "vow" and "monastery" (*votum* and *monasterium*). Married men might be received into the brotherhood only if their wives had previously made a "vow of continence" or have "already entered a convent of nuns (monastery)." — This sentence sheds significant light upon the "living in obedience, without property, and in chastity" of sentence 1, as well as on the "if anyone wish to adopt this life" of sentence 3. We shall have to return to it. — Finally, it should be noted that sentence 4 clearly indicates the collaboration of men knowledgeable in the field of canon law.[24] Even stylistically, it differs noticeably from the following sentences.

Sentence 5:   is one of those sentences which begin with, "And the friars . . . shall take heed." These sentences are quite characteristic of the *Regula non bullata,* but even in our present Rule and in the Testament, they frequently introduce significant warnings. Here it is an admonition against greed. In the candidates' renunciation of their possessions, God's will ought to be sought unhindered by the egoism of men.

Sentence 6:   serves the same purpose. It seeks to keep God's activity free from human interference, but also aims at protecting Franciscan poverty. Note especially the phrase, "God-fearing persons," i.e., persons who give their advice with a respectful regard for God. God's will is to be "sought" in individual cases;[25] it cannot be regulated.

Sentence 7:   Cursorily mentions reception into the novitiate with a view to giving directives for the clothing of the novices. The gentle moderation evident in these prescriptions regarding clothing is striking. The ministers, for their part, have the power if the occasion demands, to modify these directives — again, with a view to God's will. For it might at some time happen that God would have it otherwise than as the prescription of the Rule directs.

Sentence 8: The year of probation — the nature of which is not mentioned since this was no doubt left to practical implementation — comes to a close with profession.[26] The form of profession is likewise passed over in silence, although already then, as today, profession was made "into the hands" of the superior. On the other hand, the contents of this profession are clearly indicated. Profession is the promise "to observe always this Rule and Life." Hence, it is not confined to the three vows, but is co-extensive with life according to the Rule. Whoever promises this is "received to obedience." Profession, therefore, is not reception into a monastery or cloister, but reception into a relationship of obedience. The one making profession is received into the "realm" of obedience. This spatial image is characteristic of Francis. He preferred to speak of obedience in terms of a friar "going beyond obedience," "straying outside obedience," "standing firm in obedience," and never speaks simply of something against obedience.[27] Just as the monastery was the "place" where the monks of ancient monasticism lived their lives, so obedience is the "place" where the Friars Minor are to live their lives. The friar enters this realm when he consents to and accepts as obligatory the way of life which he has made his own during the year of probation.[28]

Sentence 9: shows that this promise is irrevocable. Because there is question here of life in the kingdom of God, this irrevocability stands sealed with the word of the Lord cited from the Gospel (cf. Lk 9:62). In addition, it is confirmed by a special decree of the Church.

Sentence 10: The professed are again described as those "who have already promised obedience" — those who through their profession have willingly entered into a relationship of obedience; hence, those who are in fact willing to live in this obedience. Then a directive on the clothing of the professed is given. This directive conforms, even more explicitly than that given for novices, to the Gospel norms addressed to the Lord's disciples when He sent them out on their preaching mission. This Gospel injunction, in fact, was the normative model for the evangelical life of the Friars Minor.[29] Like the disciples sent out by the Lord, the friars too are to have only one piece of clothing, and no foot wear except in case of necessity. If it appears more in harmony with God's will, however, i.e., if God can give His blessing and approbation, then the clothing of the professed may be less austere than is actually set forth in the Gospel paradigm.

Sentence 11: Voluntary poverty should not lead to arrogance: it should not make a friar proud of his achievement. With such an attitude, poverty itself would become a possession, albeit a possession of an immaterial sort, in which the possessor, i.e., the man boastful of his poverty, indulges his own pride. This would certainly not be that poverty in spirit which the Lord demands of His disciples in the Sermon on the Mount (Mt 5:3). In the urgent plea of this sentence of the Rule, Francis manifests his concern about the practical living of this evangelical poverty. His friars must not be Pharisees who pass judgment on the rest of the world from their pedestal of poverty. Their poverty should become — a most profound insight! — the means to honest self-knowledge and self-criticism. For this reason, sentence 11 ranks among the key sentences of the Rule for the attitude of a Friar Minor. Its deepest meaning is hard to grasp and still harder to realize in life. — Further, this admonition suggests that the food of the friars was ordinarily far from "dainty." Unlike, e.g. the Rule of St. Benedict,[30] our Rule says nothing more about the matter. Apparently there was as yet no need to.

Let us pause briefly here for a survey of the literary structure and contents of sentences 3 to 11. Sentences 3 and 4 give positive admonitions about reception into the brotherhood; sentence 5 adds a pertinent negative warning. Sentences 4, 7, and 8 describe important events in the life of the brotherhood; sentence 9 again adds a corresponding negative admonition, this time in the form of a prohibition based on a two-fold motivation. Sentence 10 simply enumerates in four statements, each beginning in the Latin with the word *et,* what is obligatory and what is permissible; sentence 11 gives appropriate cautionary admonitions. As an analysis of the *Regula non bullata* would easily show, we have before us here a manner of presentation typical of Francis. And it is precisely this manner of presentation which indicates that in the Rule Francis has his eyes fixed on spiritual values. Specifically, in these first groups of sentences he is quite clearly concerned with "living in conformity with the holy Gospel" and "living in conformity with the holy Roman Church." The impression is there that Francis takes up only such matters in the daily life of the friars as call for incorporation into the form of life prescribed by the Gospel and the Church. What to his scrutinizing eye does not require such integration is simply passed over. It needs no "regulation."

Sentences 12 and 13:   Can be considered together in our analysis. Very clearly and quite in contrast to those in the *Regula non bullata,* they set forth liturgical norms for the new way of life in terms of the Divine Office and of fasting — the "worship of God" as P. J. Olivi regards these prescriptions in his commentary on the Rule.[31] First of all, it should be noted that the sequence: reception into the brotherhood — clothing of the friars — praying the Divine Office — fasting — is found not only here but also, and in identical order, in the *Regula non bullata*[32] and in the Testament.[33] Its presence here is further witness to Francis himself as author of the Rule, even though it must be granted that the incorporation of the Office and of fasting into the life of the Church at large in the form here presented is due to outside collaboration, both juridically and stylistically. Yet, even here, there is an unmistakable respect for the thought and expression of Francis himself on the part of his collaborators. This is evident especially from the final sentence, namely, that the friars are not obliged to observe corporal fasts in time of manifest necessity. Any jurist commenting on this "time" of necessity would have defined its exact meaning and spelled this out in detail. But Francis evidently left it up to the conscience of his individual brothers. For, as will be shown later, at that time the only superior was the minister provincial, and he obviously could not always be immediately at hand for consultation.

Sentence 14:   With this sentence we now arrive at the basic core of the Rule — the infusion of spirit into the concrete "life of the Friars Minor." The clause, "when they go out in the world," is decisive for any understanding of the Rule. Here and in what follows, Francis had in mind his friars as they went about on their travels, in bigger or smaller groups, as wandering preachers or as part time preachers and laborers — not sedentary men, but active apostolic men[34] whose friary is the whole world.[35] Now he gives them, point by point, completely practical instructions for their life on the road.

With a solemn urgency and a genuinely biblical style that recalls some of the exhortations of St. Paul, Francis proceeds to bring the conduct of his friars into conformity with the Gospel way of life — their conduct towards each other as well as towards the world about them — first negatively, then positively. They are not to quarrel nor dispute nor judge others. Rather, they are to be meek, peaceful, modest, gentle, and humble. In a word, they are to act as genuine *minores* on their journeys and attend to their apostolate. As St. Francis saw it, courtesy too belongs to this *minoritas,* for he adds that on their journeys the friars should be courteous to everyone they meet.

Sentence 15:   As true Friars Minor, they are not to journey on horseback. In Francis' day, travel by horse was the privilege of the nobility and the wealthy. The Friars Minor, therefore, were not to go about in the world like aristocrats and rich people, but like the little people, the *minores* in the society of their day.

Sentence 16:   Whenever they enter any house on their journeys, the friars are to extend the greeting of pace which the Lord himself gave to His disciples when He sent them out on their mission. Their coming to men should always be in the service of peace.

Sentence 17:   Once they have found a place to stay, they are not to burden their host with special requests. They should simply eat whatever is set before them without concern about some possible monastic custom to the contrary. They enjoy the same freedom which the Lord imparted to His own disciples when He sent them on their mission. God at His own good pleasure would freely provide for His messengers through their fellowmen. Again, sentences 16 and 17 correspond almost word for word with the Gospel pattern of the life of the Friars Minor (cf. Lk 10:5, 8). The Gospel which marked the beginning of Francis' new life[36] was powerfully at work also in the formation of his Rule!

Sentence 18: sets forth a restriction that was important for Francis and his age. The friars are not to accept money, even when it is offered to them: "that they by no means receive coin or money." As we learn from the *Legenda,* lodging at people's homes, especially in the cities, was one of the prime occasions already at that time for people to offer monetary alms.[37] St. Francis, accordingly, issues a strong prohibition, again taken from the Gospel message (cf. Mt 10:9), which brooks no exception. Here Francis once more manifests his concern for *minoritas.* In his day money meant security for the present as well as for the future, because money still had its own inner value and was always exchangeable. The *minores* of medieval society had no money in this sense. At that time money was not yet the conventional means of exchange paid out in representative sums for work done. Rather, money was real investment, capital equivalent to what at present might be termed productive resources. Today, by way of contrast, we never know the true value of our paper money; we simply take it at its face value and use it as a conventional and functional means of exchange and trade.

Sentence 19: The "nevertheless" marks off the positive admonition. The superiors are to exercise a special concern for their brothers in proportion to their needs in a given situation. As expressly emphasized here, this is a personal responsibility incumbent upon the superior. Their thoughtful solicitude for all the needs of the friars should set aside all possible pretexts to transgress the prohibition concerning money.

Sentence 20: From the very beginning manual labor or, more

specifically, work for a daily wage provided another means for the "bodily support" of the friars. As the friars worked alongside the people, they exhorted them to Christian living.[38] Here Francis gives them an ever valid directive about how they should relate their work to their life as religious.

Sentence 21a.   Manual labor also offered the opportunity to earn money. For this reason an admonition relative to the "payment for their work" follows immediately.[39] The wages for their labor may not consist in money but only in "natural goods," as was the custom among the daily wage earners, the *minores,* of medieval society. Furthermore, the work must be done for the good of the *fraternitas*: for "themselves and their brethren." Again, as a token of their *minoritas,* they are to request their wages "humbly as becomes the servants of God and followers of most holy poverty." Here also Francis intends to shape the concrete life of the friars with the right attitude. As Friars Minor they may lay no legal claim to a wage and may accept only what is needed for their daily sustenance. The next injunction follows immediately from this.

Sentence 21b: The friars may not earn more than they need to live on: "whatever is necessary for the bodily support of themselves and their brethren." Work then, as today, was the way to ownership of property, and this was by no means an infrequent goal even among religious Orders in the Church.[40] Sentence 21b, accordingly, sets down a negative restriction to what was positively conceded in sentence 21a. The words "receive" and "appropriate" in sentences 21a and 21b are corelative terms. The friars are not to become good wage earners. Their work is not to lead to the ownership of property, which gives security, as in the older Orders. Neither should their services be requited with property, as was often customary in the feudal system of those days. This prescription of the Rule, then, seeks to prevent the work of the friars from becoming a means of accumulating capital; for this reason it prohibits the acquisition of property in any form.

Sentence 22:   pursues the subject even more urgently. All the friars but especially those who work, are to remain conscious of the fact that in this world they are to serve the Lord as pilgrims and strangers. The "serving the Lord" in sentence 22 corresponds to the "servants of God" in sentence 21a. Pilgrims and strangers have no permanent home; they must be poor and humble. And they ought not to be ashamed, when the occasion arises, to beg for alms with trust in God's providence.[41] The example of Christ in the Gospel should be their inspiration.

Sentence 23: Because this way of life is hard and burdensome, now the negative elements give way to the positive in the form of a solemn pleaful hymn to that "sublime height of most exalted poverty." This sentence contains a whole biblical theology of poverty unexcelled for its brevity yet fullness of expression. Filled with unbridled enthusiasm, Francis reveals in this hymn the deepest reason for all that he had previously said to the friars about their way of life, and at the same time points out to them the meaning of their life of poverty in salvation history. It is the way to the kingdom of God.

Sentence 24: Here Francis once more turns his gaze to the wandering groups of friars, the pilgrims and strangers who have no permanent home. Wherever they might be or whenever they might meet one another on the road, they are to "treat each other as members of one family" — a very touching expression. They are to be "at home" in their mutual love. Brotherly love must substitute for house, homeland, and friary at all times and in all places. The mention of a mother's love for her child, which the friars are to surpass with their love for one another, emphatically underscores what is said. In this more than motherly love of the friars for each other, each friar, even though he be without a home and without a country, is to feel secure and at home.[42]

Sentence 25: touches upon a related but special case: "if any friar falls *in infirmitate*" — thus in the original text! Hence, if any sick friar falls, i.e. collapses to the point of becoming bedridden so that he cannot continue the journey with the others, then the others should care for him as the Golden Rule of the Sermon on the Mount demands (cf. Mt7:12).[43]

Sentence 26: considers the case of one of the friars sinning gravely, i.e. becoming sick in soul, while on a journey. He is to turn back immediately; to run back as fast as he can to the minister who had sent him out, and to seek healing from him "to whom care for the souls of the friars is entrusted."[44] If the minister is a priest, he should attend to the sinful friar himself; if not, then the healing should be imparted by a priest-friar of the Order.[45] Thus the spiritual remedy should be imparted within the *fraternitas.* But once more, not according to the prescription of law, but with a regard for God: "in the sight of God."

Sentence 27:   gives both an admonition and an exhortation relative to this brotherly service. It must be free from all imperiousness, carried out in true *minoritas* but also in genuine *fraternitas,* in true brotherly love.

With this sentence, the first series of directives for the concrete everyday life of the friars (sentences 14 to 27) comes to an end. As has become clear, the series is not logically structured. Rather, Francis follows his friars step by step on their way through the world, admonishing and exhorting with fatherly concern. In all he says, his chief interest is that they remain always and everywhere *fratres* and *minores.* At the same time, his directives give us valuable insights into the life of the friars of those days, the life which the Rule was to "regulate," i.e. preserve in the right spirit.

Sentence 28:   With this sentence Francis begins his description of the organizational elements of the brotherhood. Why he does so precisely at this point is not easy to say. We might offer the following conjecture. In his thoughts Francis is so intent on following the sinful friar on his way back to his minister provincial that he simply loses sight for the moment of the other friars. And so the "ministers provincial" now occupy his attention, since they had just been the subject of sentences 26 and 27. Francis, accordingly, now speaks of the other duties of these same ministers. Undoubtedly, the most important of these tasks is to elect the minister general of the entire Order. Therefore, sentence 28 first of all prescribes that the entire brotherhood should always have one of the friars as common superior.[46] He is to be a "brother among brothers." His office is one of service to all. The description of his office is drawn from the Gospel (cf. Mt 20:25-27). Here "minister and servant" is not a title but a statement defining the scope of his office, just as "general" has nothing to do with being a "general" in any kind of military sense, but rather means that he is the duly qualified minister of the brotherhood in general. As "minister general" the "whole fraternity" is entrusted to him. This distinguishes him from the "ministers provincial" who have responsibility only for the friars in their own territories. Again, in contrast to the organization found in monastic Orders, all the friars throughout the world owe obedience to the "minister general." The circle of obedience that goes out from him encompasses and unifies the whole fraternity. He stands at the center of this circle; he is the "head of this Order," as Francis calls him in the prologue of the earliest Rule.

There is a further interesting fact to be pointed out here, namely, that the Rule speaks only once of a task of this minister general, even though at this time, as history testifies, a minister general had highly centralized plenary power concentrated in his hands.[47] Sentence 32 of the Rule mentions almost incidentally that it is the duty of the minister general to appoint qualified friars to the office of preaching, and that is all. Thus while the minister general, so to say, seems freed from obligations, the ministers provincial, on the other hand, are given directives and commands for various duties (even a command "by obedience," cf. sentence 40). However, this is not really so surprising when we recall that Francis himself held the office of minister general when the Rule was composed. It would have been rather incongruous for Francis to admonish himself in regard to his own office! Besides, throughout the Rule, Francis has his eyes fixed on the "life of the friars," which he follows with his admonitions. And when he comes to treat of the "ministers of the friars" here, he — as an admonishing observer — simply does not see himself as part of the scene! Only toward the close of his life, when the question of his successor became acute, did he seek to fill this obvious lacuna in the Rule with that "description of the minister general" recorded in 2

Celano 185-186. Significantly, St. Clare later incorporated a passage from this description into her own Rule to define the tasks incumbent upon the office of Abbess.[48] Furthermore, this lacuna in the Rule points emphatically again to Francis as the author of the Rule. In any other supposition, such an oversight would certainly have been detected either by the Roman Curia or else in the Chapter!

Sentence 29: indicates, first of all, that the minister general keeps his office for life. After his death a successor is to be chosen by the "ministers and custodes," i.e. by the provincial ministers, at the Chapter of Pentecost.[49] This Chapter, as a rule, is to take place every three years. The agenda for these Chapters, when no election is held, is not specified. Evidently this was well "regulated" in practice. Therefore Francis felt no need to say anything about the matter, just as he is equally silent about the manner of election and all other related questions. Because there were as yet no acute problems in this area, he simply passes over the whole question in silence and leaves it to the future.

Sentence 30: The ministers provincial are referred to now also as the "custodes"[50] and rightly so, since this sentence confers on them the right to supervise the minister general's manner of fulfilling his office. The right belongs to the ministers provincial as a body, but nothing is clarified regarding the juridic status of this "body of the ministers provincial" or how the whole group is to fulfill its duty practically and effectively in a satisfactory manner. — If the whole group of the ministers should be of the conviction that the minister general is no longer acceptable for the service and general welfare of the whole fraternity, then they have the right and duty to elect another "as custos." Again, "custos" is a general term designating an office; but it does offer a clear insight into the meaning of the office of superior for the wandering preachers of the Order. It is important to note that the ministers are to exercise the right ascribed to them here only with a view to God: "in the name of the Lord"; hence, not influenced by human respect or Order politics. As so often elsewhere in the Rule, the liberty granted the friars (here, the ministers) is guaranteed and safeguarded not from a juridic but from a religious point of view, by being related and subjected to God. For Francis, this relationship to God is a stronger and more living bond than any pertinent and factual reference to norms of law. It is precisely this consideration that raises the strongest objections to the thesis that the Rule was the work of the Roman Curia. It simply bears too clear a witness to the Christian spirit of the saint and an entirely different approach.

Sentence 31: Upon returning from the Chapter of Pentecost, the ministers provincial may, if it seems advisable to them, convene *all* the friars "in their custodies," i.e. in their own provinces, for a Chapter. The provincial Chapter, therefore, like the preceding genuinely "general" Chapter in the Order, ought to be an assembly of *all* the friars together with their minister. On this occasion the minister provincial would have the opportunity to inform his friars about everything that was considered and decided at the general Chapter. For this reason, the provincial Chapters were to take place "after the Chapter of Pentecost." This sentence adequately describes the purpose and significance of the provincial Chapters for the practical life of those days. They were to facilitate a unity of outlook between the "whole fraternity" and the "fraternity in each province." These Chapters served as the spiritual framework for both the internal and external life of the Order.

Sentence 32: For us today the transition from sentence 31 to sentence 32 is quite abrupt. Yet it is not really so if we keep the concrete circumstances of those times in mind, as Francis does here. At the end of the Chapter, the friars were re-assigned; new groups were formed, the area in which to pursue their apostolic work was designated, and the friars set out on their missions. It is precisely in this context that Francis gives his exhortation. The friars are to exercise their apostolates only in subordination to the hierarchy of the Church and as commissioned by their superiors. This negative directive is then followed by:

Sentence 33: the positive directive. The preaching of the friars should be shaped by their *minoritas*, i.e. it should be without fancy

rhetoric; it should be well thought-out, straight-forward and brief;
it should be as simple as the Lord's words in the Gospel. Their
preaching should also be a brotherly service directed to the up-
building of the kingdom of God in others, i.e. serving the practical Christian life with a view to man's last end.

Sentence 34:   Francis again turns to the friars on the road
engaged in the mission entrusted to them. They remain under the
care of those who, as their servants and ministers, have responsibility for them. Hence Francis again speaks of the duties of these
ministers. The minister is to give his undivided attention to his
friars, to visit them and, as an ancient chronicle observes: "to
console the friars by his visits."[51] He is to go about cheering up
and encouraging the friars wherever they might be.[52] And it is
precisely on such occasions that they ought to meet with the friars
as their "lesser brothers," i.e. giving exhortations and directives
"humbly and charitably" as their "little ones" (*minores*) and
brothers (*fratres*) and, so to say, bolstering as well as strengthening
the bond of obedience that binds them all to one another. For
this reason obedience is to have only one purpose — to serve the
Christian life of the individual and of the group in conformity
with the Rule. In this lies its breadth and, at the same time, its
limitation.

Sentence 35:   Such obedience is possible only when each friar
who is a subject (there is, therefore, a necessary and genuine subordination!) continually looks to God and is always ready "for
God's sake" to renounce all self-will. The obedience of the friars
functions within the framework of their profession. For this reason
they are implicitly charged with the responsibility of judging
whether their obedience tallies with and preserves the "life of the
Friars Minor" as described in the Rule.[53] That this is the sense
here is shown clearly in the sentence that follows.

Sentence 36:   The minister and servant cannot be in all places
at the same time. Therefore when a friar on his travels comes into
a situation that makes living according to the spirit of the Rule
impossible, he must — regardless of the "obedience" given him —
have recourse to his minister in all haste (*recurrere* — to run

back!). And the minister is to "receive" him with kindness and love. His attitude must be one of "familiarity" toward a brother without a home or homeland of his own. The minister's love, kindness, and readiness to be of service should invite genuine recourse. Every minister is to be a servant ready to help any friar because he considers each of his brothers as his master.

Sentence 37: What has been said in the three previous sentences simply defies all human comprehension. Therefore, sentence 37 now follows with its unfathomable and profoundly Christian exhortation to conquer all egoism, especially all self-glorification.[54] As with the other spiritual admonitions of the Rule (sentences 11, 14, 23), the directives set forth here must also be understood both within the context of the individual case to which it refers, i.e. the situation described in sentence 36, as well as in an all-inclusive sense. The concrete situation at the same time provides the basis for a more general admonition. In reading this exhortation, both aspects must be kept in mind.

Sentence 37a: approaches the matter first negatively. The friars are to be on their guard against all "pride, vainglory, envy, and avarice, of care and solicitude for the things of this world, of detraction and murmuring." Hence, in the case in question, i.e. the case presented in the Rule, the minister is not to act arrogantly when a troubled brother comes to him; and the latter is not to be proud but to make known his need, his perilous situation. Neither of the two should let their encounter be influenced by considerations of human respect, "vainglory." There is also no place for that greed which seeks to justify one's own opinion or preserve outward appearances at any price. No one should envy or scold another or broadcast his faults (*murmurare* — to prattle about!) All these are sinful attitudes which Francis wants to see eliminated above all in treating with a sinful or troubled friar.[55] But they are also entirely incompatible with the demeanor of a Friar Minor in general. For all these sinful attitudes are the expression of human egoism, the sign of an ego focused upon itself and, therefore, turned away from God. This attitude is the "spirit of the flesh," as Francis was wont to call it,[56] which in the Christian must be replaced by the "Spirit of the Lord." It is only from this perspective that the last warning in this sentence can be rightly understood, viz. no one is to adopt an attitude of superiority towards others because of scholarly learning, or in any way use his scholarly achievements as a wedge against others.[57] All this would make it impossible for the friars to live together as *minores*. Hence all the friars are committed to the obligation pointed out in:

Sentence 37b: positively. All the friars are to strive above all to possess the "Spirit of the Lord, and His holy operation," i.e. all are to be open to the Spirit so that He may be able to work through them. His activity shows itself first of all in prayer coming from a pure heart, in the prayer of a man forgetful of self and totally directed towards God, entirely devoted to Him.[58] The Spirit of the Lord works best in a person who preserves humility and patience in all adversities, such as persecution, sickness, blame, and reproach. As has been pointed out, what occasioned this great exhortation is specifically the relationship between superior and subject. But here in this list, this specific situation merges into a farther reaching, general objective! — Last but not least, the Spirit of the Lord manifests Himself in love for one's enemies. Love for one's enemies belongs in a special way to a life formed by the Gospel, as is shown by the Scriptural texts with which Francis brings this admonition to a close.

Sentence 38:   This admonition aimed at governing all interpersonal relationships is followed, as in sentences 14 and 23, by several directives, sober even in their grammatical construction, for life "on the road." Under no circumstances shall the friars have suspicious dealings or conversation with women (38a). They also shall not enter the convents of nuns, unless the Apostolic See has given certain friars a special mandate to this effect (38b). Finally, they shall not involve themselves with any family ties or obligations deriving from kinship, not even under the seemingly pious pretext of being a godparent (38c). In short, the friars should remain totally free for their particular calling, as Thomas of Celano so poignantly describes the vocation of Francis: "he went about in the cities and villages . . . he announced the kingdom of

God, proclaimed peace, and preached salvation and penance for the remission of sins."[59] Nothing was to deter the friars from fulfilling this task which the Church had entrusted to them.

Almost needless to say, the three directives of sentence 38 also have a special import as safeguards for "living in chastity."[60] In this sentence Francis expressly warns the friars of the dangers that can confront them on their journeys in regard to this particular facet of their Gospel life.

Sentence 39: The farthest and most dangerous journeys are made by those friars who go to mission lands to work among non-Christian peoples. Francis will not simply send a friar on such a journey without further ado. Rather, it was his conviction that the vocation of such missionary friars demanded a special calling on the part of God, a particular "divine inspiration," as well as a special approval and commission on the part of the competent superior.[61] The friars departing for their missions receive no special directives for their apostolate. They simply and evidently are, above all, to put the witness of their totally Christian and evangelical lives at the service of the kingdom of God, the same as any other friar was expected to do on a journey.

With this the saint's glance has, so to say, scanned the horizons of the way of life and the apostolate open to the friars of his own day. With fatherly love and care he has said all there was to say, all that he deemed necessary for the journey through their "Life." And so the Rule ends here; its goal has been achieved.

Sentence 40: The practical everday life of the friars has been "regulated." There follows now a final all-inclusive exhortation to underscore indelibly the fundamental purpose of the Life of the Friars Minor, the "tenor of our life," which was so comprehensively set forth in sentences 1 and 2. This final exhortation cannot refer only to the sentences immediately preceding but reflects back on everything that went before. "Finally," i.e. "in addition to all that has been said" (Latin: *"ad haec"*), Francis adds the following: The friars must be firmly anchored in obedience to the Church, which they encounter in the person of the Cardinal Protector. He is to be the "governor, protector, and corrector of this fraternity," in effect its highest superior; the "Pope of the Order," as Francis himself expressed it on one occasion.[62] The duty to request a Cardinal Protector from the Lord Pope at any time rests upon the ministers, perhaps on the ministers assembled at the time of the General Chapter. Here, too, a legalistic obscurity prevails! — It is the duty of the Cardinal Protector to keep the friars constantly within the structural life of the Church through unswerving obedience and steadfast faith. Only then can they realize the goal of their life, the substance of their profession, namely, to preserve the poverty and humility of Christ which are the keystone of a life lived according to the Gospel.[63]

We shall certainly not go wrong in seeing sentences 1 and 2 together with sentence 40 of the Rule as the decisive statements which permeate everything else in the Rule with spirit and life. They contain the first and the final expression of that purpose which must give meaning to all individual points of the Rule. If this arrangement of the Rule is verified the testimony of the biographers of St. Francis: "he placed the holy Gospel above all other considerations" (2 Celano 216). Between these two appeals to a commitment to the Gospel life, like two clamps holding firm everything they enclose, all the individual details of this life are given a spiritual unity. They form three great thought patterns built upon a structure of concrete association: Sentences 3 - 13 treat of the internal growth of the fraternity, of the external manifestation of its life, and of its liturgical worship in the service of God. Sentence 14 initiates the section (14-27) which instills "spirit" into the concrete everyday "life" of the friars. Sentences 28 - 39 follow with a second series of admonitions and exhortations which seek to instill this same "spirit" but in a different context. Sentence 40 summarizes all that went before in a final all-inclusive exhortation.

In retrospect, then, we may conclude our analysis with this observation: The Rule contains what its title had promised, "Here begins the *Life* of the Friars Minor." We were able to learn and better understand the "Life of the Friars Minor," first the internal life and, through this, the external life as well.

NOTES

1. Contrary to both critical editions, the beginning of the Rule should read as follows: "In the name of the Lord! Here begins the life of the Friars Minor." The words, "In the name of the Lord!" were a common introductory phrase affixed to a written document, as is evidenced by many medieval manuscripts. As such, it was also familiar to Francis (cf. *Regula non bullata* 4; *Opuscula* 29; *Analekten* 4) and, in addition, is completely in harmony with his belief in God as the sole cause of all things (cf. Esser, *Franziskus und die Seinen*, Werl 1963, 38ff). The phrase loses some of its characteristic meaning, therefore, by combining it with the following heading of the Rule, viz. "In the name of the Lord begins the Life of the Friars Minor." The German translation in *FranzQuellSchrift* I, Werl, 1963[3], 80, rectifies the matter.

2. There is evident here a new element in comparison with the *Regula non bullata*, which is a very valuable witness for the real direction of this development and, therefore, for the homogeneity of this fact, as his dream of the small pieces of bread from which he was to make a host indicates (2 Celano 209 in *Omnibus of Sources*, p. 529; the *Regula non bullata, ibid.*, pp. 31-53.)

3. For the following, consult the section: "Der Name des neuen Ordens," in Esser, "Ordo fratrum minorum. Über seine Anfänge und ursprünglichen Zielsetzungen," in *FranzStud* 42 (1960) 116-118. — This study presents the basic historical data for our analysis to which we shall repeatedly refer. Since it has appeared in two successive volumes of the aforementioned periodical, the page numbers are not uniform. For this reason, we shall refer to it by chapter and section number (viz. I, 3 = Chapter I, Section 3).

4. Cf. Esser, "Ordo fratrum minorum," II, 2 (112); *Order of St. Francis*, 76 pages (Franciscan Herald Press).

5. Esser, "Franziskus von Assisi und die Katharer seiner Zeit," in *ArchFranchHist* 51 (1958) 263.

6. Esser, "Mysterium paupertatis. Die Armutsauffassung des hl. Franziskus von Assisi," in *WissWeish* 14 (1951) 177-189. Eng. trans. *Repair My House*, Franciscan Herald Press, Chicago, 1963, pp. 73-92.

7. *Regula et Constitutiones generales Ordinis fratrum minorum*, Rome 1953, passim. — The text of the Rule contained in the edition of the *Constitutiones* likewise retains the textual errors noted in footnotes 24 and 25 above.

8. Cf. the account published by Boehmer (*Analekten*, 85f) drawn from ancient sources. It makes this matter very clear. For the problems set forth there, cf. Esser, *Das Testament*, 161f; 16.

9. Cf. the section: "Das schnelle Wachstum des neuen Ordens," in Esser, "Ordo fratrum minorum," II, 6 (125-128).

10. For interesting examples, cf. the Bull "Quo elongati" of Gregory IX (cf. note 7 above), as well as the *Expositio quatuor magistrorum super*

regulam fratrum minorum (1241-1242), which Livarius Oliger O.F.M., has critically edited (Rome 1950). Hugo of Digne, in his explanation of the Rule (*Speculum Minorum,* P. III, fol. 32va-35va) shows himself better informed historically, yet also offers evidence for our statement.

11. Cf. the section: "Die ersten Krisen und Versuche zu ihrer Überwindung," in Esser, "Ordo fratrum minorum," IV, 1-2 (171-215), where in the "Conclusions" (214f) this aspect is particularly set in relief.

12. Elmar Wagner O.F.M., *Historia constitutionum generalium Ordinis fratrum minorum,* Rome 1954, 172-175.

13. For "rule and life," cf. Esser, "Ordo fratrum minorum," V, 2 (318-322).

14. Cf. the section: "to live in conformity with the holy Gospel," in *art. cit.,* V, 2 (314-323).

15. Cf. Esser, "Mysterium paupertatis," 177-189; *idem,* "Bindung zur Freiheit. Die Gehorsamsauffassung des hl. Franziskus von Assisi," in *WissWeish* 15 (1952) 161-173; *idem,* "Freiheit zur Liebe. Keuschheit und Jungfräulichkeit in der Auffassung des hl. Franziskus von Assisi," *ibid.,* 19 (1956) 100-108. (Eng. trans. of all three, cf. footnote 6 above. — These studies show that Francis always conceived the counsels from the fullness of biblical thought, and that juridical and moral questions were treated by him as entirely marginal.

16. K. Esser, "Die religiösen Bewegungen des Hochmittelalters und Franziskus von Assisi," in *Festgabe für Joseph Lortz,* Vol. II (Baden-Baden 1957) 287-315; *idem,* "Sancta Mater Ecclesia Romana. Die Kirchenfrömmigkeit des hl. Franziskus von Assisi," in *WissWeish* 24 (1961) 1-26 (Eng. trans. cf. footnote 6).

17. *Regula non bullata,* Prologue (*Opuscula* 24, *Analekten* 1); cf. also 2 Celano 185: "head of the Order of the Poor" (*Omnibus of Sources,* p. 510).

18. *Regula non bullata* 2 (*Opuscula* 26, *Analekten* 2).

19. *Regula non bullata* 2: "If anyone moved by divine inspiration wish to adopt this life"; *Testamentum* 4: "Those who came to adopt this form of life" (*Opuscula* 25 and 79, *Analekten* 2 and 37).

20. Francis had earlier handed over this plenary power to other friars as well (cf. Jordan of Giano, Chronicle 11, *Legenda trium sociorum* 41). Yet these "delegations" are expressly said to be temporary.

21. This holds true even for the extremely detailed Benedictine Rule: "St. Benedict presupposed many things which are unknown to us today," B. Steidle, O.S.B., *Die Regel St. Benedikts,* Beuron 1957, 150, 235, 237.

22. Cf. *Werkbuch zur Regel,* 145-148; there the historical background of these demands is shown in detail. (Eng. trans. footnote 19, chapter II).

23. The full extent to which Francis understood this concept is shown in Esser, "Mysterium paupertatis," 179-182. (Eng. trans. footnote 6).

24. Sentence 4 is obviously formulated according to the Canon Law of those days; cf. *Decretum Gratiani:* "If a married man wishes to enter a monastery, he is not to be received unless he has first been freed from

his marriage bond by a profession of chastity on the part of his wife" (c. 22, CXXVII, q. 2); cf. also the decision of Pope Innocent III (1198): "Nor may one party turn to the Lord and the other party remain in the world; moreover, one of the spouses may not be received to regular observance unless the other spouse has made a promise of perpetual continence. The other partner must also change his or her way of life, unless perhaps due to his or her age, that partner can remain in the world without suspicion of incontinence" (*Decretal. Gregorii IX*, c. 13, III, 32); cf. also the decision of Pope Honorius III himself: "and is of such age that no suspicion can be raised against her, but you shall not allow her to be forced against her will to enter a convent and observe a vow of continence" (*Decretal. Gregorii IX*, c. 18, III, 32). The tenor and terminology of the Rule are unmistakably influenced by these decrees. A clear transition from a "profession of chastity" and a "promise of continence" in the earlier decrees to the "vow of continence" in Honorius III, is also evident. The earlier Christian profession here becomes a vow!

25. For sentences 5 and 6 of the Rule, cf. *Werkbuch zur Regel*, 147-150. (Eng. trans. footnote 19, chapter II).

26. For sentences 7 and 8, cf. the section: "Novitiate and Profession," in Esser, "Ordo fratrum minorum," IV, 2a (183-188).

27. *Ibid.*, II, 3 (315).

28. Cf. the section: "To go beyond obedience," *ibid.*, IV, 1b (174-176).

29. *Ibid.*, V, 2 (318).

30. *Regula s. Benedicti*, Chap. 39-41.

31. P. J. Olivi, "Expositio super regulam beatissimi patris Francisci," in *Speculum Minorum*, p. III, fol. 111ra.

32. Chap. 2 and 3 (*Opuscula* 25-29, *Analekten* 2-4).

33. *Testamentum* 4 (*Opuscula* 79, *Analekten* 37).

34. Cf. the section: "Migrant wandering preachers," in Esser, "Ordo fratrum minorum," III, 1 (297-301).

35. *Sacrum commercium beati Francisci cum domina paupertate*, n. 63, where the Friars Minor of Lady Poverty wend their way through the whole world while saying: "This is our cloister, our lady." The *Sacrum commercium* dates most probably from 1227, hence, before 1 Celano; it is therefore a very valuable witness for early Franciscan life; cf. Esser, "Untersuchungen zum 'Sacrum commercium beati Francisci cum domina paupertate,'" in *Miscellanea Melchor de Pobladura*, Vol. 1, Rome 1964, 3-7.

36. 1 Celano 22 (*Omnibus of Sources*, pp. 246-247).

37. Cf. *Legenda trium sociorum*, 40 (*Omnibus of Sources*, 39, p. 928).

38. Cf. Esser, "Die Handarbeit in der Frühgeschichte des Minderbrüderordens," in *FranzStud* 40 (1958) 145-166.

39. In his Testament (n. 5) as well, Francis speaks of wage labor ("to receive wages") and demands it of all his friars, (*Opuscula* 79, *Analekten* 37f).

40. This thought turns up repeatedly in that great speech of Lady Poverty, which forms the central portion of the *Sacrum commercium*

(n. 37-51). It was, therefore, thoroughly familiar to the early generation of Franciscans.

41. This connection between sentences 20-23, which also harmonizes with other sayings of St. Francis, should never be overlooked. It is precisely in this passage that the careless division of the Rule into chapters proves a source of many misunderstandings; cf. Esser, "Die Handarbeit," 157.

42. For a further explanation of sentences 21b-25, cf. the section: "To live without property," in Esser, *Franziskus und die Seinen,* 97-132. But this treatment too does not look to the "Sitz im Leben" of this statement of the Rule.

43. Cf. Esser, "Ordo fratrum minorum," III, 1 (300).

44. *Regula non bullata* 4 (*Opuscula* 30, *Analekten* 5).

45. It was an ancient monastic custom to confess one's sins to the superior. Many statutes of various Orders demanded this also for grave sins already confessed to another priest; cf. P. Browe, S.J., "Die Kommunionvorbereitung im Mittelalter," in *Zeitschrift für kath. Theologie* 56 (1932) 387 and 398ff.

46. Cf. for what follows, the section: "The common superior for all," in Esser, "Ordo fratrum minorum," III, 2 (301-315).

47. *Ibid.,* 304ff.

48. Description of minister general in *Omnibus of Sources,* pp. 509-511; Rule of St. Clare, IV, 8 (*FranzQuellSchrift* II, 95).

49. The original Chapters of the Friars Minor, referred to in the Rule in sentences 29-31, are described in the section: "The regular Chapters," in Esser, "Ordo fratrum minorum," III, 3 (316-326). They are not to be equated with today's General and Provincial Chapters.

50. In the Rule, "minister and custos" still represents the descriptive function of an office holder in the Order; the expression, therefore, should not be interpreted in the sense of later titles for officials in the Order. Proof for this may be found in Esser, "Ordo fratrum minorum," III, 2 (312f).

51. Jordan of Giano, Chronicle II; cf. also note 5.

52. Cf. "Visitation and recourse," in Esser, "Ordo fratrum minorum," III, 4 (326-329). — Precisely here one must be on guard not to interpret the concepts in their later juridical sense. They are still to be understood entirely in terms of concrete life.

53. St. Francis' conception of obedience would correspond fully with the will of the Pope today; he expressly stated: If obedience signifies the offering of one's will, yet it ought to be demanded only "within the limits of charity and with regard for the dignity of the human person" (Paul VI, "Allocutio ad summos Moderatores," *art. cit.,* 535a).

54. For a detailed exegesis of the following sentence, 37a and 37b of the Rule, from the viewpoint of the spirituality of St. Francis, which is indispensable for the understanding of his spiritual concern in these decisive statements, cf. *Werkbuch zur Regel,* 238-246 (Eng. trans. footnote 19, chapter II).

55. Cf. *Werkbuch zur Regel,* 205ff (Eng. trans. footnote 19, chapter II).

56. Cf. Excursus 2 (*"Leib"* and *"Fleisch"*) and 4 (*"Geist," "geistlich"*) in: *FranzQuellSchrift* I, 197-199 and 202-206.

57. Admonitio 7 (*Opuscula* 10, *Analekten* 44).

58. Cf. Excursus 1 (*"rein"* and *"Reinheit"*) in *FranzQuellSchrift* I, 194-197; there this concept, so central for St. Francis, is explained in its full scope.

59. 1 Celano 36 (*Omnibus of Sources,* pp. 258-259).

60. Cf. *Werkbuch zur Regel,* 247-253, where the historical background of these prescriptions is more precisely pointed out (Eng. trans. footnote 19, chapter II).

61. Cf. K. Esser, "Gehorsam und Freiheit," in *WissWeish* 13 (1950) 142-150.

62. 2 Celano 25 (*Omnibus of Sources,* p. 383); Jordan of Giano, Chronicle 14. — For a discussion of all this, cf. Esser, "Ordo fratrum minorum," IV, 2c (210f).

63. For the full meaning of this sentence in its historical background and significance, cf. Esser, "Die religiösen Bewegungen und Franziskus," **308f.**

VI

RESULTS OF THE ANALYSIS

After our somewhat extended though necessary analysis of the text of the Rule itself, we are now in a position to draw up and summarize the results of our analysis:

1. The Rule of the Friars Minor in content and composition is a genuine work of St. Francis. Only he could have drawn up this Rule so characteristic of his thought. The numerous statements in the "I-form" (I admonish, I command, etc.), as well as the direct addresses to the friars (you, my most beloved brethren, etc.) confirm this conclusion. At the same time, however, individual passages clearly indicate the helping hand of others. Certain sections show the influence of the then current Canon Law of the Church (cf. sentences 4, 12, 13, 26 and 32), but not without a noticeable respect for the will of Francis (cf. especially sentences 13 and 26). Perhaps it is precisely here that we can surmise the knowledgeable help of Cardinal Hugolin who later personally stated that he had assisted St. Francis "in drawing up the Rule." For a number of reasons we can also exclude, it seems, any juridic contribution from the Roman Curia. Its scribes did not even trouble themselves to formulate an original introduction to the Bull of Confirmation but simply took over a formula, "The

Holy See is accustomed to grant" (*Solet annuere*), which previously had been used in granting certain privileges to the Cis-
tercians.[1] That is how seriously the Roman Curia took the young
Order as late as 1223! — Other sections of the Rule also show
the influence of a stylistic revision (cf. sentences 11, 14, 23, 33,
37 and 40). Here particular attention might center on the fact that
among these are found precisely those exhortations and admonitions which have special significance for the spirit of the Rule
and, accordingly, also for the life of the friars. Apparently those
friars who helped in the definitive redaction of the text of the
Rule placed special value on these exhortations and admonitions
of Francis,[2] whereas they left the directives concerned primarily
with externals in the more awkward style which, according to the
evidence of the other Opuscula, was typical of Francis (cf.
sentences 10, 15-17, 24-25). Because of all this, we will have to
picture the friars' collaboration with St. Francis in the definitive
redaction of the Rule in a way wholly different from what later
legend would have us believe.

The question whether these friars or the Curia had expunged
important statements of the saint from the text of the Rule, as
later legend would also have us believe, is to be answered in the
negative. For in his Testament, Francis on the one hand strongly
endorses the Rule as it stands; on the other hand, he does not
take up for consideration any of the deletions alleged in this so-
called "Protest against the Rule." Accordingly, we ought to abide
by what the original text itself indicates.

2.   As the analysis clearly shows, the Rule is not a legal work
aimed at regulating each and every aspect of life. When Francis
set it down in writing, as is also the case with his Testament, he
had the concrete life of his friars before his eyes and sought to
animate this way of life, as it had developed, with the right spirit.
From this several important consequences follow:

a.   The Rule is a spiritual document. To stress this is of the
utmost importance. The Rule is an exhortation of the saint directed
to his friars. Accordingly, nearly all the sentences of the Rule are
in the subjunctive; hence, more in the sense of a wish or a desire

than in the sense of an obligation or a command. Only four
sentences have *debe(a)nt* (15, 25, 27, 36); four *teneantur* (26,
28, 29, 30); three *praecipio firmiter* (18, 35, 38a); and one *per
obedientiam injungo* (40). Now while these words and phrases
in themselves might seem to indicate a greater obligation, this is
not borne out by a consideration of the actual matters involved,
as e.g. a comparison of sentences 15 and 18 with 21b and 40
clearly shows. In other words, the Rule at times uses juridically
stronger terminology without thereby implying greater severity of
obligation. One cannot therefore determine what the Rule seeks
to emphasize simply on the basis of these formulas.[3] For they
are the utterances not of a jurist but of a "spiritual father" who
is concerned with a way of life that is to be shaped by a totally
distinct spirit.

    b. Hence the Rule is a "form of life" and this — an im-
portant point — is the life of the friars. Their way of living stands
behind the directives of the Rule. The "Sitz im Leben" for the
exhortations and directives of the Rule is to be sought in that
concrete way of life. Hence the Rule, as St. Bonaventure had
already correctly observed, is not a presentation of the unique,
charismatic personal life of St. Francis. He did not make himself
and his personal way of life the norm and "Rule" for others.[4]

    c. Moreover, Francis takes the brotherhood's way of life as it
had developed up to 1223 with full earnestness; he seeks to give
spiritual guidelines for this way of life, commensurate with the
state of development it had already reached. Basically he does
nothing different there from what he had done previously in his
Regula pro eremitoriis[5] for those friars who desired to lead a
more meditative-contemplative life in strictly secluded hermitages;
or in his letter to St. Anthony[6] when the question of studies in the
Order became acute; or in his letter to the Chapter[7] when the
question of priests in the Order and the problem of common worship in the growing communities of the friars required solution;
or in his Testament, when the question of the houses and churches
of the friars became a burning issue.[8] Never did Francis "protest"
against any one of these developments. Rather his total concern

was always to instill into these developments the distinctive spirit of his brotherhood, i.e. precisely the same spirit that is evident in the Rule.

3. Now let us attempt to highlight the most important components of this formative spirit as presented throughout the Rule:

a. The friars are to live in the spirit of the Gospel. It is this spirit which ultimately and definitively is to shape their way of life, and this over and above the letter of the Rule. — This gives rise to the question: Should not, then, the "observe the Holy Gospel of our Lord Jesus Christ," to which we are obliged according to the Rule (sentences 1, 40), take on greater dimension for us with our present day heightened understanding of the Scriptures? And does this not apply also to our living according to the "form of the Holy Gospel?"

b. This way of life of the friars, formed by the Gospel, is to dovetail with the life of the Church always, unconditionally and with faithful obedience (sentences 2, 40). The Church is their mother[9] from whom they receive their life. — Again we must ask: Does not, therefore, the "form of the Holy Roman Church," into which the Rule wants to incorporate us so intimately, take on added dimension for us with our growing understanding of the nature of the Church, of its inward and outward life?

c. This evangelic way of life in the Church receives its specific stamp from its *minoritas* and *fraternitas,* with its view fixed as it is upon the poverty and humility of our Lord Jesus Christ (sentence 40). Hence its concern is with Gospel brotherhood, which is made possible, safeguarded and perfected through poverty and humility, and which for the friars signifies the realization of the kingdom of God (sentences 9, 23). Today, especially because of our understanding of the Scriptures, an appreciation for this specific concern of the Rule is growing in the Church. Once more we must ask: After 700 years of history so often encumbered with totally inconsequential problems, do we even now view our life in the proper perspective? Are we cognizant of the fact that our General Constitutions in Art. 204 still call the prohibition of the

Rule regarding money (cf. sentence 18) "the most distinctive precept of our Order?" Or do we conceive the "without property" of the Rule only from a material point of view, in terms of things, as the jurists certainly must do, and thereby lose the deeper meaning of the "mystery of poverty" as unselfish openness to the kingdom of God (sentence 23)?

d. Because it is concerned with the kingdom of God, the Rule also demands that spirit which respects God's freedom over all things. It aims to see that this freedom of God's is guaranteed whenever it may touch immediately on the life of the friars. The Rule does not want to interpose itself between God and the life of the friars by impeding or regulating anything in this area. The life of the friars is rather to be continually and permanently exposed to God's free rule. Perhaps because of this, Francis once called the Holy Spirit the minister general of the Order; and perhaps because of this he even entertained the idea of stating this explicitly in the Rule, but it proved no longer possible since the Rule had already been confirmed.[10] Thus where we would have expected more precise prescriptions, Francis faithfully and simply refers matters to God: "as the Lord shall inspire them," "moved by divine inspiration," "with the blessing of God," "in the sight of God," "in the name of the Lord." These and similar expressions — there are ten in all! — look to a life built on faith, which does not rivet itself to the letter of the law, but rather knows how to refer to the living and operative God in every situation. And note that it was precisely the wholly poor Francis who possessed such a rare and fine sense of the immediate activity of God in the life of men. He realized that it was precisely this which makes God the owner of all the good things in our life. Our belonging to God and the resulting firm trust in his fatherly direction are not to be constricted by law. This is no doubt the decisive reason why Francis wanted to shorten the already existing Rule! This belonging to God, through the medium of the *mysterium paupertatis,* allows God to be the Father of the friars in an entirely concrete and direct sense. Belonging to God, the friars become "men in the service of God." It is not by accident that the Rule speaks of the friars as "servants of God" (sentence 21a) and as "serving the Lord" (sentence 22), i.e. with those Scriptural terms used in both the Old and New Covenant to designate men who as servants of God belong to the kingdom of God. It is precisely these Biblical terms and what they entail that precludes the idea that Francis is here adopting an attitude which allows everyone the freedom to do as he pleases. The individual belongs to God as His personal possession; and this fact only heightens his personal responsibility to make a continually fresh decision for God and His kingdom. And he can and must make this commitment. Thus what is involved here is the individual's genuine freedom to serve God. In this service of God by the friars their genuine freedom, as trusting and obedient children of God, is guaranteed. Their personal responsibility before God is clearly spelled out.[11]

At this point we can already say with full right that it is not the Rule which is obsolete; for it is as young and timeless as the Gospel, whose marrow it intends to offer to the friars. What is obsolete, however, are all those expositions of the Rule which — and we all sense this — disregard the "Sitz im Leben" for the directives of the Rule, and offer instead a juridical exegesis and a legal interpretation of the Rule. And, as will become even more evident, it is precisely in fashioning such an interpretation, that they miss the real meaning of the Rule.

4. After what we have set forth thus far, it will come as no surprise to state that the Rule does not describe a monastic, cloistered way of religious life. It has nothing to do with the cloistered life of a monastic community, but is concerned with religious life of a totally different character, namely, religious life as set forth in its Gospel model. The fraternity described in the Rule is a community of men bound together personally more than locally, a brotherhood with a strongly dynamic character. It is not closed within itself, but open to the world in the Biblical sense, entirely dedicated to the service of the kingdom of God. And it remains thus in its entire way of life, not just in its outward activity (sentences 9, 23; 21a, 32). Francis even dared to identify profession of the Rule with qualification for the kingdom of God. He

tells us that whoever consents to the way of life of the brotherhood and undertakes it through profession is fit for the kingdom of God (sentence 9). Thus for Francis one does not live in God's kingdom in the closed community of a monastery, but in that personal fellowship which binds the friars together as "brothers according to the spirit," i.e. as brothers united by the Spirit of the Lord; which binds each to the other (sentences 24, 37b); and which binds all together in their service to men. Therefore, they appear in the Rule as groups of itinerant preachers or preaching laborers (sentences 14, 20, 32). Like the first apostles of the Lord, they too are on the road as pilgrims and strangers; and their goal is the kingdom of God (sentences 22, 23).

5. Yet the kingdom of God can be made present in the fraternity only to the extent that the individual friar adopts, appropriates and substitutes the "Spirit of the Lord" for the "spirit of the flesh," i.e. all egoism, self-glory and self-will — hence, to the extent that each individual becomes a "brother according to the Spirit" in the sense set forth in the Rule (sentences 37a, 37b). This calls for penance or conversion in the Gospel sense of *metanoia* — a change of heart and mind. But such *metanoia* is possible only in poverty, in the "will-to-have-nothing," in being poor outwardly but above all inwardly (sentences 11, 14, 23, 37). Granted the full significance of outward poverty, yet the decisive thing here is inward poverty, a selflessness that extends to and is operative in all things. It is precisely this which makes room in men's hearts for the "Spirit of the Lord and His holy operation" (sentences 37a, 37b).

The history of the Order teaches through many and often alarming examples that it is important to stress the aforementioned point. A cult of outward poverty without foundations sunk deep in inward poverty simply leaves open the door to a dangerous liberalism and individualism, coupled with arrogance and pride in one's external achievements. Often enough this sort of poverty led not only to separation from the Order, but to heresy and apostasy from the Church. From the perspective offered by history, we can readily see the fundamental significance of sentence 37 of the Rule.

For this reason Francis never considered poverty an ultimate value. It always has a subservient, protective and facilitating function. It is the way to Christian brotherhood in selfless love, as is clearly indicated by the connection between sentences 23 and 24. In terms of salvation history, poverty is the way to the kingdom of God.

6. For this reason, too, the Friars Minor do not form themselves into cloistered monastic communities, dependent upon common property as a means of sustenance. Their means of sustenance are rather: the hospitality of the people at whose homes they stay while on their preaching journeys (sentence 17); the special help of "spiritual friends" (sentence 19); most of all their own work (sentence 21a); and, when these fail, then the begging of alms (sentence 22). According to the Rule, the Franciscan fraternity does not consist of small communities dependent on begging as their means of support in such a way that they are to live from begging alone. According to the Rule, therefore, the Order of Friars Minor is not a mendicant Order in the strict sense.[12] And this is even less the case at present, because especially today every Friar Minor, including those actively engaged in some apostolate, can contribute through his "work" to the support of all. Those engaged in the care of souls as well as those who pursue scholarly studies in the Order no longer need begging as a sort of "benefice" from which to provide for their needs as in the Middle Ages. Indeed, today perhaps more than even in the past, our fraternities still rest upon an insecure poverty which, precisely because of its insecurity, summons each friar to renewed personal effort and diligence in working for his confreres (sentence 24). From this vantage point, poverty should also be considered as insecurity of existence which guarantees brotherliness. The fraternities of the Friars Minor once again appear as groups of brothers bound together in personal, not local, fashion. — The foregoing consideration especially makes it quite clear that in the observance of their Rule, the Friars Minor should not

be bound to social and economic conditions which no longer exist. Rather their efforts must be seriously directed to living the Rule according to its spirit and in line with today's economic and social conditons. Otherwise the Order would launch itself on a flight from historical reality.

7. Therefore, the apostolic work of the Friars Minor is not limited by a "stability of place." The friars are to make their way through the world with open eyes and to work for God's kingdom wherever their work is needed. But they are to do so in the realm of obedience into which they have been received through profession (sentence 8). This obedience alone provides their non-cloistered life with a bond without which no common brotherhood could exist. This relationship of obedience, however, does not have a domineering role. Rather, in line with the Gospel, it has a subservient character (sentence 36), because it is rooted in the whole mystery of poverty, i.e. safeguarded by a constant view to Christ's obedient poverty, to the *"exinanitio Christi,"* cf. Phil 2:5ff (sentences 37a, 37b).

8. In our Rule, the following appear as elements *shaping* the Franciscan type of community: 1) A common cult, carried out in closest conjunction with the life of the Church. This common worship is the salient feature of the friars' life together; it is the source of this way of life and gives it its distinctive character. Hence the Rule speaks of it before all else in the practical life of the friars (sentences 12, 13). 2) Secondly, a very special form of obedience which no friar may renounce lest he be unfit for the kingdom of God (sentences 8, 9). 3) Thirdly, the feeling of being "at home" in the mutual love of brothers who are filled with the Spirit of Christ — a love greater than that of a mother (sentence 24). 4) And, finally, the *familiaritas,* the family atmosphere which binds especially superior and subject to each other (sentence 36). All four elements once again show the brotherhood of the Friars Minor to be a community bound together not by proximity in space, but by strongly personal ties.

9. In the Rule, the following come to hand as elements *preserving* the Franciscan type of community: 1) clothing, the

same for all, simple and above all inexpensive, yet also distinctive so that the friars on their journeys — "wherever any of the friars may be and shall meet other friars" — may recognize one another (sentences 10, 24); 2) a common superior for all the friars, through whom their life is bound in obedience to the Church, and in whom they are bound together "everywhere in the world" (sentences 2, 28, 34, 40), and to whose representative in a given territory (province) the friars owe equal obedience (sentence 34); 3) the Chapter, to be held regularly; above all, in the individual provinces, the Chapter — understood as the assembly of all the friars with their minister — is to serve the common way of life of the brotherhood (sentences 29, 31); 4) and, last but not least, the Rule itself, which aims to preserve the life of the friars as true *minores* with its genuinely Spirit-filled directives.

10.   Consideration of the Rule as an element preserving the Franciscan type of community leads us to a further aspect which shows us how little Francis was concerned, even in the Rule itself, with juridical institutions. The many examples presented in our analysis have shown us how Francis at times presents positive admonitions along with corresponding negative warnings, or vice versa, and thereby reveals and in fact sets up a double polarity of life. Between these two poles the concrete everyday life of the friars must be lived. Now the realities of daily life are marked with varying shades, which are too elusive to be fixed with any sort of precision, certainly not with legal precision. If Francis does in fact leave this double polarity open in a sort of confident carelessness, and thus places upon his friars the task of making repeated personal decisions for God, he shows how well aware he is of the deepest concern of Gospel freedom. He wants to assure this freedom as much as possible for his friars.

11.   In the Rule only provinces are mentioned as the friars' proper place of living. The corresponding superiors over these areas are the provincial ministers, the servants and ministers of their brothers. Their obligations include concern for the healthy continuation of the brotherhood (sentence 3), care for sick friars as well as those in need for other reasons (sentence 19), solicitude

for sinful or otherwise imperilled friars (sentences 26, 36), the assignment of duties as well as the commissioning of friars for their apostolates (sentences 31, 39). Upon their convening for the Chapter of Pentecost, the ministers as a group bear the responsibility for the common welfare of the whole brotherhood (sentence 30). Finally, they have the duty to ask for a Cardinal Protector as need arises (sentence 40). One may therefore say that what the abbot was for ancient monasticism, the minister provincial is for the Friars Minor; what the monastery was for the former, the province is for the latter. The province is like an abbey extended over a given territory.[13] Therefore, the Rule makes no mention as yet of any other superiors beneath the ministers provincial with authority over the friars.[14]

By way of complement, we might remark here that Celano too presents the ministers provincial as the only competent superiors in the Order of his day. These ministers provincial did de facto implement their office after the model of the abbots in the years following the approval of the Rule. Then when, also de facto, Elias rightfully sought to fill the juridical vacuum of the Rule relative to the minister general — and this must be clearly stated once and for all! — the revolt of the provinces in 1239 led to his downfall and branded him as the great scapegoat of the Order.[15] Though this revolt of the provinces did definitively assure their ministers of their voting rights, and caused the minister general to lose his former power,[16] the episode only goes to prove the powerful influence of the concept borrowed from the abbacies of that time.

12. Also worthy of note is the sociological structure for the brotherhood presented in the Rule. It is totally shaped by the spirit of the Gospel, both in its vertical as well as in its horizontal lines (sentences 28, 30, 34, 35, 36). In the Rule at least, these structural patterns in no way conform to the spirit of this world, nor do they correspond to the then current legal mentality of the Church. Precisely in this lies one of the special values of the Rule and a very special characteristic of our brotherhood. The Church today, more readily disposed to relinquish the last remaining relics

of the "grant of Constantine," should have greater understanding for this point in the life of the friars than the Church of the Middle Ages. The brotherhood of St. Francis could not avoid the overpowering influence of the medieval Church, a Church held captive by feudalistic ways of thinking. In this context, it should be clearly noted that the distinction between clerics and laics, which occurs only in sentence 12 of the Rule, refers simply to a friar's ability to read and to write, and the distinction is made in the Rule merely to determine the type of Divine Office to be recited by each.[17] Hence it is not a distinction of a sociological nature, i.e. inferring the existence of two separate classes, at least not in the Rule.

13. Need is part and parcel of the life of poverty outlined in the Rule. The friars' way of life requires whatever necessity occasions, whatever is needed for all human life, whatever the Friar Minor cannot dispense with in his own life.[18] The Rule, therefore, speaks of this "necessity," of the "necessities of life," in very significant passages. Now it is striking that in all six passages where it occurs, this concept is used quite as a matter of course. In other words, it is never fixed, never "regulated," but rather obviously left up to the here and now conscience of the individual. This holds for those "who are compelled by necessity to wear shoes" (sentence 10), as it does relative to the "manifest necessity" which dispenses the friars from bodily fasting (sentence 13), and the "manifest necessity" which allows them to ride horses (sentence 15). This is made even clearer in cases when superiors are obliged to care for their friars "as they may deem necessary" (sentence 19), or when the friars are given the right to accept "whatever is necessary" for themselves and their confreres as payment for their work. That "needs" will arise is recognized. Yet there is no legally determinable norm given to cover these situations; no precedents are set. Individual cases must be solved as they arise.

The freedom which this entails, because it is not juridically determined, could naturally be abused and lead to one friar using more than another, or allowing himself more than another. And this in turn could lead to social inequality, to social distinctions of a purely worldly nature in the way of life of the friars. That many a friar did not escape this danger is shown by the history of the Order. To ward off this danger, therefore, unfortunately "only" one admonition of the Rule sets forth an obligation in conscience in this regard (sentence 24). This obligation is expressed very unjuridically, yet quite clearly and emphatically. Every friar is to anticipate the "needs" of his confreres with even more than a mother's love. The life of the friars together, their meetings with one another, should be marked by a genuine and mutual give and take governed only by necessity. They are really to have and use everything in common, in openness to the needs of others. Each one, in the spirit of poverty and with the will "to-have-nothing," "to-keep-back-nothing-for-oneself," is to make the personal effort to provide whatever might relieve the need of his confrere. In this way all desire for possessions, all greed which seriously threatens Gospel brotherliness in the life of the Church as well, should be eliminated from their way of life in common. If all the present indications are not deceptive, then the post-conciliar Church will not only require this witness of our life but most ardently anticipate it as well.

All in all, we can recapitulate as follows. In the Rule which he gave us, Francis was most deeply concerned with the practical implementation of the "life of the Friars Minor." And the basic meaning of that "life of the Friars Minor" is this: to bear witness to Christian brotherhood as the realization of the kingdom of God.

NOTES

1. Esser, *Das Testament,* 178, note 154; *idem,* "Ordo fratrum minorum," III, 2 (313, note 54).

2. In *Werkbuch zur Regel,* 43-45; 67-68, Lothar Hardick O.F.M., has already made deeper research into the style of the Rule. (Eng. trans. footnote 19, chapter II).

3. Cf. Hardick, *ibid.,* 46-52; however he interprets these expressions of the Rule too much from the later, more juridical point of view. (Eng. trans. footnote 19, chapter II).

4. With this statement we follow closely the text of the Rule, without

presuming to determine the extent to which Francis may be considered or factually was the *"forma Minorum,"* in the sense of the ancient antiphon ascribed to Card. Thomas of Capua (d. 1243); cf. *AnalFran* X, 387. On the whole matter, cf. also Esser, "Ordo fratrum minorum," III, 5 (337, note 37).

5. *Opuscula* 83f, *Analekten* 68. — K. Esser, "Die 'Regula pro eremitoriis data' des hl. Franziskus von Assisi," in *FranzStud* 44 (1962) 383-417. — All the questions connected with the "stability of place" of the Friars Minor, which go beyond our Rule text, are treated together in: Esser, "Ordo fratrum minorum," IV, 2b (188-201).

6. *Analekten* 71. — K. Esser, "Der Brief des hl. Franziskus an den hl. Antonius von Padua," in *FranzStud* 31 (1949) 135-151.

7. *Opuscula* 99-107, *Analekten* 57-62.

8. *Opuscula* 80, *Analekten* 38. — Esser, *Das Testament,* 172-174.

9. Esser, "Sancta Mater Ecclesia Romana," 5-10. (Eng. trans. footnote 31).

10. 2 Celano 193 (*Omnibus of Sources,* p. 517).

11. Cf. L. Hardick, *Werkbuch zur Regel,* 63. From his study he draws the following conclusion: "From all this follows a very strong assurance of opportunities for free, personal decisions. That this could be expressed within the framework of a religious Rule must be qualified as astounding. A comparison with other religious Rules . . . would certainly make the whole import of this statement apparent. One must keep in mind that the Rule of the Friars Minor is unique in this . . ."

12. Cf. on this important question: Esser, "Ordo fratrum minorum," V, 4 (340, especially 344, note 44).

13. B. Koltner O.F.M., De juribus Ministri provincialis in Ordine Fratrum Minorum usque ad annum 1517, Rome 1961, 22-25.

14. For the origin and early development of the office of local superior, cf. Esser, "Ordo fratrum minorum," IV, 2c (201-205).

15. Cf. *ibid.,* III, 4 (329, note 12).

16. Heribert Holzapfel O.F.M., *Handbuch der Geschichte des Franziskanerordens,* Freiburg i. Br. 1909, 173.

17. Lothar Hardick O.F.M., "Gedanken zu Sinn und Tragweite des Begriffes 'Clerici'," in *ArchFrancHist* 50 (1957) 8-26.

18. Bernardus de Bessa, *Liber de laudibus beati Francisci,* in cp. 4, "De paupertate," gives a penetrating analysis of the concept of "necessity" for the life of poverty; cf. *AnalFran* III, 674.

VII

CONCLUDING THOUGHTS

The Rule, then, is concerned with a way of life. Its aim is to shape the concrete life of the Friars Minor as lived up to 1223 in the spirit of the Gospel and, thus formed, to incorporate it into the life of the Church. It does this in a most unique way, which juridically is certainly unsatisfying but, viewed in Christian perspective is excellent. For this reason, this Rule is *not to be lived juridically,* but to be ventured upon, *to be risked,* in Christian faith. The Rule itself intends this risk, as is evident especially from its constant references to the "divine inspiration" and to the "needs" of the friars, both of which present a direct challenge to be open to this risk. For this reason our way of life must always be concerned with this risk encountered in the spirit of the Gospel, in the "Spirit of the Lord and *His* holy operation" (sentence 37b).

That the risk is hazardous requires no proof. A host of personal experiences tells us so only too loudly. But whether one *may* avoid the risk through ever more voluminous constitutions and statutes must first be ascertained from the spirit of the Gospel. And whether one *can* avoid the risk through ever more extensive laws must be determined from the history of the Order. And whether growing legalism is not a greater danger, leading ultimately to a new Pharisaism, is a question which we, with many of the Council Fathers, ought to ask again today.[1]

In the course of our considerations, we have surely all noticed that our life in the Order today, in many of its concrete features, is much the same as the life of the first friars or at least tending back in that direction. Pastoral work and the apostolate, the manifold needs of the Church and of the kingdom of God, have demanded and shaped for us a way of life that continually clashes with a cloistered, monastic way of living. In fact, today our way of life increasingly threatens to break away from those medieval patterns of behavior which the Order, for reasons necessary at that time, had assumed in the 13th century. Should this change be judged as something purely negative? Or should we not rather face the fact — in line with our considerations — and ask ourselves: Do we not have, because of these changed circumstances, the unique chance to let the Rule again become incarnate in our lives? Do not our changing times now allow us to live once more in harmony with the spirit of the Rule in its original sense? Could we not let this everyday life of ours be "regulated" in a totally new way through the spirit-filled directives, the fatherly exhortations and warnings, the solicitous commands and prohibitions, which Francis gave his friars for their way of life?

Francis never "protested" against what was necessary for the life of the Church in his day. Nor should we, for the sake of the past, "protest" against what is necessary for the life of the Church today. Rather we should strive to vivify the life of the Church today in and with the spirit of our Rule. We simply may not dare to stifle the demands of the Church at present with the patterns of behavior from an irretrievable past. To do so would be to fail in that obedience to the Church which the Rule rightly demands from us.

Furthermore, if the Rule did not regulate everything that was in fact regulated simply by the ordinary daily life of the friars, and if the saint left to the future many things in basic need of regulation, have we not then also the right and duty to regulate and animate our present concrete way of life in this way, just as Francis had done in his Rule for the Order's state of development in 1223?

Today as always, our task must simply be to adjust our concrete life as shaped and required by the life of the Church to the "form of the Holy Gospel" as the Church understands it. In other words, today even less than before, our goal cannot be a repetition of one of those always basically fruitless attempts to observe the Rule "to the letter."

Looking back on our considerations, if we have rightly interpreted the signs of the times in the Church of today, then we, as no other generation in the history of the Order, have the possibility and the duty to accomplish what the Rule, in sentence 36, so very much wanted to see safeguarded and protected: "to observe the Rule spiritually." Perhaps such a life according to the Rule in its original sense will rekindle in us enthusiasm for the genuine and authentic *"Life of the Friars Minor."*

NOTE

1. Pope Paul VI also warns religious in responsible positions in their Orders against such a continually growing legalism which can offer no salvation: "it often happens that, the more norms that are legislated, the less the spirit is drawn to their observance. Hence, in making laws, General Chapters ought always to exercise the power they enjoy with moderation and with prudent judgment" ("Allocutio ad summos Moderatores," *art. viti.,* 536a-b).

Part II
THE TESTAMENT

I

THE TESTAMENT OF ST. FRANCIS

This is how God inspired me, Brother Francis, to embark upon a life of penance. When I was in sin, the sight of lepers nauseated me beyond measure; but then God himself led me into their company, and I had pity on them. When I had once become acquainted with them, what had previously nauseated me became a source of spiritual and physical consolation for me. After that I did not wait long before leaving the world.

And God inspired me with such faith in his churches that I used to pray with all simplicity, saying, "We adore you, Lord Jesus Christ, here and in all your churches in the whole world, and we bless you, because by your holy cross you have redeemed the world."

God inspired me, too, and still inspires me with such great faith in priests who live according to the laws of the holy Church of Rome, because of their dignity, that if they persecuted me, I should still be ready to turn to them for aid. And if I were as wise as Solomon and met the poorest priests of the world, I would still refuse to preach against their will in the parishes in which they live. I am determined to reverence, love and honor priests and all others as my superiors. I refuse to consider their sins, because I can see the Son of God in them and they are better than I. I do this because in this world I cannot see the most high Son of God with my own eyes, except for his most holy Body and Blood which they receive and they alone administer to others.

Above everything else, I want this most holy Sacrament to be honored and venerated and reserved in places which are richly ornamented. Whenever I find his most holy name or writings containing his words in an improper place, I make a point of picking them up, and I ask that they be picked up and put aside in a suitable place. We should honor and venerate theologians, too, and the ministers of God's word, because it is they who give us spirit and life.

When God gave me some friars, there was no one to tell me what I should do; but the Most High himself made it clear to me that I must live the life of the Gospel. I had this written down briefly and simply and his holiness the Pope confirmed it for me. Those who embraced this life gave everything they had to the poor. They were satisfied with one habit which was patched inside and outside, and a cord, and trousers. We refused to have anything more.

Those of us who were clerics said the Office like other clerics while the lay brothers said the *Our Father,* and we were only too glad to find shelter in abandoned churches. We made no claim to learning and we were submissive to everyone. I worked with my own hands and I am still determined to work; and with all my heart I want all the other friars to be busy with some kind of work that can be carried on without scandal. Those who do not know how to work should learn, not because they want to get something for their efforts, but to give good example and to avoid idleness. When we receive no recompense for our work, we can turn to God's table and beg alms from door to door. God revealed a form of greeting to me, telling me that we should say, "God give you peace."

The friars must be very careful not to accept churches or poor dwellings for themselves, or anything else built for them, unless they are in harmony with the poverty which we have promised in the Rule; and they should occupy these places only as strangers and pilgrims.

In virtue of obedience, I strictly forbid the friars, wherever they may be, to petition the Roman Curia, either personally or through an intermediary, for a papal brief, whether it concerns a church or any other place, or even in order to preach, or because they are being persecuted. If they are not welcome somewhere, they should flee to another country where they can lead a life of penance, with God's blessing.

I am determined to obey the Minister General of the Order and the guardian whom he sees fit to give me. I want to be a captive in his hands so that I cannot travel about or do anything against his command or desire, because he is my superior. Although I am ill and not much use, I always want to have a cleric with me who will say the Office for me, as is prescribed in the Rule.

All the other friars, too, are bound to obey their guardians in the same way, and say the Office according to the Rule. If any of them refuse to say the Office according to the Rule and want to change it, or if they are not true to the Catholic Faith, the other friars are bound in virtue of obedience to bring them before the custos nearest the place where they find them. The custos must keep any such friar as a prisoner day and night so that he cannot escape from his hands until he personally hands him over to his minister. The minister, then, is strictly bound by obedience to place him in the care of friars who will guard him day and night like a prisoner until they present him before his lordship the Bishop of Ostia, who is the superior, protector, and corrector of the whole Order.

The friars should not say, this is another Rule. For this is a reminder, admonition, exhortation, and my testament which I, Brother Francis, worthless as I am, leave to you, my brothers, that we may observe in a more Catholic way the Rule we have promised to God. The Minister General and all the other ministers and custodes are bound in virtue of obedience not to add anything to these words or subtract from them. They should always have this writing with them as well as the Rule and at the chapters they hold, when the Rule is read, they should read these words **also.**

In virtue of obedience, I strictly forbid any of my friars, clerics or lay brothers, to interpret the Rule or these words, saying, "This is what they mean." God inspired me to write the Rule and these words plainly and simply, and so you too must understand them plainly and simply, and live by them, doing good to the last.

And may whoever observes all this be filled in heaven with the blessing of the most high Father, and on earth with that of his beloved Son, together with the Holy Spirit, the Comforter, and all the powers of heaven and all the saints. And I, Brother Francis, your poor worthless servant, add my share internally and externally to that most holy blessing. Amen.

NOTE: This translation of the Testament was made by Fr. Benen Fahy. It is taken from the *Omnibus of Sources,* pp. 67-70.

II

CONVERSION OF FRANCIS
(Section 1)

It was Vatican Council II that posed the question of their own identity to the various religious communities. We know how often the Council spoke about the "propria indulis," the unique character of religious communities, and how the Council purposely protected this unique character of each congregation. Today one feels how comprehensively vital the question is for individual congregations; it is not only a question of "What are we doing? What must we do?" but "Who are we? What are we really in the Church?" I feel that this is a very healthy question for all action must grow out of our own being, and therefore in response to the suggestion from your General Council, I believe it is good that we hold a series of conferences about the uniqueness of our community as a *Franciscan* community. We would like to begin with a document in which Francis speaks to us very personally and without any external influence — in his Testament.

This Testament is a spiritual exhortation through which he wishes to strengthen his Brothers in their way of life and in their vocation as well as all others who will follow him. The Testament is a document of what Francis really lived totally. In it he takes a backward look and speaks of his whole life, of that which he wanted particularly to impress upon their hearts in earnest exhortation and also by strict mandate, but above all through his own example. One can see with full clarity in this writing a witness of the fatherly love and care with which Francis cherished even unto his deathbed all his children, present and future, those near-by and those far away. Therefore we should accept this document with great reverence and attentive love, heeding these final words of the Father of our Order. We should consider these Spirit-enlightened and spirit-enlightening words of our departed Father with an inner joy. I firmly believe they can help us to find answers to many questions facing us at present. They can truly bestow spirit and life upon us as Francis himself says in the document. They can help us find ourselves and our spiritual self-awareness.

Today let us consider the first part. There we read:

"The Lord gave me, Brother Francis, the grace of beginning to do penance in this way: that, when I was in sins, it seemed extremely bitter to me to look at lepers, and the Lord himself led me in among them and I practiced mercy with them. And when I came away from them, what seemed bitter to me, was changed to sweetness of spirit and body for me. And after that I did not wait long and left the world."

One feels that in this section something crucial is being said about our own community. According to the Rule of the Third Order Regular we are called a Brotherhood of Penance. What does that imply? Here Francis gives us a truly definitive answer. Let us follow the words exactly as they come. One notices that the Testament begins with a backward glance. In utterly simple words Francis speaks of a certain mystery within his own life, of his conversion, of his beginning a life of penance. The sentences are so simple and the words so unpretentious that we are always in danger of passing over them too rapidly. Yet, whoever will meditate often on their meaning will look astounded into a world which, we must honestly admit, is strange to us today. As it reveals itself more and more to us, we realize that this is none other than God's world, the world which is "other" than that to which we are accustomed, a simple and yet so happily God's world which includes only re-directed persons as Francis here describes. "When I was in sins, it seemed extremely bitter to me to look at lepers, and the Lord himself led me in among them and I practiced mercy with them."

Let us take the words one after another. The first two sentences begin very differently than would be customary for most persons. Francis does not start out by saying: "Thus did I, Brother Francis, begin to lead a life of penance; namely, I went to the lepers . . ." but rather the exact opposite: "The Lord gave me, Brother Francis, the grace of beginning to do penance in this way," and "the Lord himself led me in among them." (Here I would say in parenthesis: "The Lord has called me into community life; the Lord has placed me in this work . . ." and often is added, "but it doesn't satisfy me anymore, so I will leave.")

To ponder over this awareness — not I, but the Lord — is, I believe, very important for us. The Lord has "turned" me and he has led me in His way. Only those who have experienced it speak of owing everything to God, to the Lord. Nothing good is due to one's own doing but all is the work of God. One can also say we are confronted here with the life story of the completely poor to whom the untiring God gives what God himself is. As Francis expressed it in another context, he could not be a thief in the treasury of the Lord.

The life of penance, as Francis here recalls, is a turning away from self and a turning toward God in an attitude of thankfulness. It does not have its beginning with persons, not even in wishing well for others; it has its beginning in God. In this life He is the one and only reality. This realization is the requisite beginning and, at the same time, the constantly growing fruit of conversion, of a life reversed. With this beginning the conversion of Francis was sealed, as Thomas of Celano, his first biographer, precisely describes it: "He turned his back on himself and directed his gaze totally toward God."

This being turned in another direction is conversion. Putting one's person at the disposition of God is so completely other that it is in exact opposition to the order established by man who, because of sin, would make himself the ruling principle.

With similar simplicity Francis then speaks of another very real and definite truth. This conversion, this reversal, is accomplished not somewhere and somehow in a purely spiritual realm; it is not a matter of the intellect alone nor of the will alone, nor is it pure piety or pious feeling. A reversal of person is a turning toward God, the beginning step. Letting oneself be placed at the disposition of God is accomplished in the concrete, however, in meeting with people. The decision for or against God takes place, we might here mention, not in the room for pious exercises, in the church or in the chapel, but in contact with people who are in need. As Francis writes, "when I was in sins, it seemed extremely bitter to me to look at lepers." From a purely human standpoint this is understandable. The malodorousness of body, and often also of soul, of broken men, invited truly no intimacy from others. Besides, there was always the danger for still healthy members. Loathing and aversion were aroused and each believed himself to be right and to be using good judgment when he gave wide berth to lepers. Thomas of Celano reports that the young Francis always made a big detour when he happened to come upon one of these miserable creatures; furthermore, he held his nose because he could not tolerate the stench of such persons. It was truly unbearably nauseating for him. But here is the crux of the matter: the Lord himself led him among them. God, whose grace had long drawn the young Francis, one day placed a leper in his path. He put the decision directly in front of the young man: to leave the world that was his up until then, to leave the life he had known and enter into God's world, the world of the Lord, where it is said, "All that you have done for these the least of my brothers, that you have done unto me; and whatsoever you have not done for the least of them, that you have not done for me." The decision into which the Lord led the young Francis was truly not easy. It demanded the total person. With body and soul he must throw himself into the guiding hand of God through this, up until then devastating, situation.

What would have been the result if Francis had followed his purely human inclination? We can easily answer that question today. But in that moment itself, Francis "practiced mercy with them."

The wonder of grace had fulfilled itself. This one to whom grace with proffered left everything behind him. He let himself be conquered. He did what a person would never of himself do in such a situation — but he did what God desired him to do: he had pity on them.

Francis, totally and without consideration for himself, surrendered himself completely to God and His guiding Will because he would be the servant of the Lord; in so doing he did what his Lord had done. Through the selfsame action as that of the merciful Lord, Francis was transformed into a new and completely different person. He became the man of conversion, of redirection, of penance; in him was realized what the Lord himself said as, washing the feet of his disciples, He demonstrated by this humble service that "I have given you an example that you also do as I have done. Truly I say to you, the servant is not greater than the Master, nor the messenger greater than he who sent him. Now that you know this, happiness will be yours if you act accordingly." Francis did it and was completely filled with happiness: "And when I came away from them, what seemed bitter to me, was changed to sweetness of spirit and body for me." He had put himself body and soul into his decision. The resistance in body and soul he submitted to God; and therefore body and soul experienced the happy change in his actions. The joy, mercy and love which he showered on the poor streamed back upon him. The transformation had begun. The purely human world, the mundane thoughts and sentiments, the self-centered world of sin-burdened mankind remained behind. Life in the totally-other world of God began.

With utter simplicity the story concludes: "And after that I did not wait long and left the world." Whoever would truly adhere to God and, as imitator of the Lord, would be conquered by Him through merciful love — and this is what Francis experienced in his meeting with the lepers — can no longer live as he formerly did. Therefore Francis left the world, that is, his former way of life, his milieu in which men acted on a purely humanistic level. His turning to the way of penance, following the path of returning all to God, had begun. Everything that pertained to the world he left behind.

In regard to that world, we cannot deny that the people and the milieu of the young Francis were definitely Christian; they wanted to be Christian and yet they used the world in an ordinary and human way. That was and is today the greatest peril for Christianity. As long as the Christian loves himself more than God, he will seek himself more than the kingdom of God. The so-called world will remain in us as long as our hearts will not let themselves be turned to acts of love which have their origin, their direction and their goal in the God of merciful love.

A reversal of direction! Francis left the world, the worldly appeal of his environment, the mundane thoughts and hankerings of his heart — we know how tremendously pleasing it all had been to him — and began a life of penance, a life of a converted person, a life in God's world as the Lord showed it to him. He submitted to the providence and guidance of the Lord without consideration of himself, his health, his success or the opinion of others. Thus we can now say that he was the converted man, the servant of God who was happy to do without any uncertainty of heart what the Lord commanded him. Trusting in God he now traveled an entirely new road. Just as love found him obedient, "the Lord himself led me," so obedience impelled him to love, "and I practiced mercy with them." Thus he left the purely human world to obey God totally and without reserve, to live completely in God's world. And how this happened, and how it has to happen in our lives, he reveals to us in his Testament where he praises the merciful God uninterruptedly and thanks Him for this his life shortly before his departure for the next life, before his death which he now goes to meet in all its fullness.

There is hardly a section of the writings of St. Francis that gives us such an exact and precise description of the life of penance as that on which we have just meditated together. If we had nothing but these words according to which we, as members of the Franciscan Order, are called to live a life of gospel penance, we would still have that in which it is all contained.

Yet we ask ourselves, is there anything in these words that applies to our life today; does Christ's gospel message of conversion itself in some way affect the form of our daily lives as religious? We were also called by God to a life of penance; we accepted the habit of Francis in order to do penance. This was expressed in the clothing rite used at the time of our investiture. In order to lead a life of penance, we obligated ourselves by vows to a life according to a Rule of the Franciscan Order. The Lord called us to this and along with the vocation He gave us the grace. Now the Lord expects that we will live according to this vocational grace. Therefore, if we seek an identity we need simply say that we wish to follow for our whole lifetime the gospel call to penance, to change, to conversion.

Is it not the Lord, who, time and again, stands in our path, who brings persons into our lives — not lepers necessarily as he did for Francis — but persons in need, persons in danger, persons who need our help? It can be that it is hard for us to help just these particular persons — Francis encountered them as lepers — a sick or clumsy person, a mentally depressed person, someone whose manner is unpleasant or whose total mien is repulsive to us. It can happen that it is irksome to us to help persons who really get on our nerves. We often believe also that we have something more important to do. Our own preference runs along other lines and we have other plans, or we feel that no one can expect that from us; Francis could have truly said the same in every instance. How many reasonable excuses could he not have given? Can we say of each needful person whom God places on our path that "I had pity on him; I tried to help him." Do we visualize this life of penance as God does, which is so entirely different in that we harken to what God is asking of us here and now in the persons we are encountering; not only heeding but rather obeying, doing what the Lord expects of us voluntarily and without consideration of ourselves?

At this point you will notice that we are faced with an answer to a question which is often debated today — the question of vertical versus horizontal piety, i.e., a piety which relates to God directly and a piety which proves itself through relationships with others. However, we also notice that for Francis there was no question of either-or but rather of something that was interrelated. "The Lord himself led me in among them and I practiced mercy with them." The redeemed person is always the obedient person who in every situation is ready to serve the other (this is the horizontal) in obedience to God (that is the vertical). The one does not exist without the other. Each would be an illusion without the other. We find it here expressed by Francis in so simple and yet so profound a form that we really don't have to discuss it. We will be persons redeemed, and in our communities the kingdom of God will be realized to the extent that we allow the Lord to direct us and to guide us in and through all things.

"The Lord gave me . . . the Lord led me . . . and I practiced . . ." With that everything is really said. We must let ourselves be guided and directed by the Lord to the extent that we conquer ourselves and submit ourselves, as Francis here says, with the total strength of our body and of our soul to the will of God. We must reject all that is not God, all that is of this world, leave behind us all egocentricism, all self-centeredness, in order to love God and be available to his guiding and directing Hand.

I believe that in this observation we have the first and most important requisite for finding the identity of our community. We should be Brothers and Sisters of Penance as it says in the Rule of the Third Order; this is the wish of the Church who approved this Rule.

Conversion toward penance means living in a different manner than was customary since everything is changed from what formerly was. This requires a new direction of our value system and of our value judgments. This means asking again and again, what does the Lord want of me here and now; it means that I carry it out, not so that it can be attributed to me as an accomplishment or credited to me for a reward, but rather that the Lord can work through me as He wishes so that his Will is accomplished in all things. If we would think all of this over, it would be very clear to us that conversion-penance is not a one-time act for us that remains in effect thereafter; no, conversion-penance is a new task each day and, I must admit, a difficult new task each day because there is something in it that always goes against us — "what seemed bitter to me" — and because we will always find new excuses to avoid this difficult demand on us. That is why what seems bitter to us has not yet changed to sweetness of body and of spirit for us. Perhaps we must pray still more for the grace of total conversion and genuine penance. Perhaps, in order to effect this interior and exterior conversion, we must let ourselves be still more deeply immersed in the sacrifice of Christ wherein God demonstrates to us daily the fullness of his mercy. Perhaps we must give careful attention to recognizing the grace of God present in every practical possibility in our daily lives, especially in the so-called "little things," as opportunities which at the same time accomplish anew our conversion while demonstrating its genuineness by our actions. That is, perhaps, the most important admonition that Francis gives us as he looks back at the progression of his own conversion: greatness must prove its authenticity in littleness.

Everything that leads us to God must lead us to loving service of our fellowman. How we stand in truth before God can only be recognized through our actual relationship with our fellowman. We are truly converted only when God's love and mercy are genuinely evident in our love for one another and our mercy toward one another. We have first left the world then when we forsake and disregard our own plans and our own will and seek the inspirations given by God.

The more earnestly and sincerely we obey him, the more will we be leading the life of penance desired by the Church. Then perhaps will we experience the truth of what Francis here says to us: whoever gives of himself entirely to God's love and renders unreserved mercy toward all persons with whom he comes in contact, without consideration of himself, finds in God's love true joy. God's world, the kingdom of God, let us be clear on this point, is the happiest world; it is that which makes us truly joyful for precisely here, in God's world, in God's kingdom, the ancient saying is fulfilled:

"Happy is he who, forgetting himself, brings another happiness. Joyful is he who, without calculating the cost, brings another joy."

That is true; and that it can and will be so in our own lives is guaranteed us by our holy Father St. Francis not only by his words here in his Testament, but particularly through the witness of his entire life. The more we become a fraternity of penance, the more will we become a community of happy persons in God's Church.

III

FAITH IN CHURCHES
(Section 2)

The next section of the Testament of St. Francis that we wish to consider reads:

"And the Lord gave me so much faith in churches that I prayed and said simply thus: 'We adore you, O Lord Jesus Christ, here and in all your churches all over the world, and we bless you because by your holy cross you have redeemed the world.' "

In the first part of his Testament Francis described his conversion in a faith-filled unpretentious manner. Two points became obvious to us in our consideration: first, Francis saw in his conversion the work of God who led him along a path which, in human terms was neither intelligent nor planned for the future. I would like to insert here that I believe we would not have so many departures if we were convinced of this fact: that it was God who converted us, who led us into a new way; that it was God who guided us along a way that had absolutely nothing to do with intelligence and future planning in human terms — and then to persevere in this road of God's. Secondly, Francis' conversion took place in meeting with suffering mankind, precisely with lepers, to whom Francis showed the same merciful love that God had shown him.

The conversion of Francis is, essentially, this: he acted according to his realization that before the merciful love of God, which is a gift, all our supposed rights to self-assertion and all our claims upon others melt away like snow in the sun. Since God's love has shown mercy toward us sinners, we must also behave toward others with merciful love, selflessly and without reservation. That is the transformation of persons and of the world which takes place repeatedly since the Incarnation and Passion of the Son of God, and which was realized so completely in Francis that for him nothing remained the same as it had been. Therefore he left the world as he says at the end of the first paragraph of his Testament, to give himself unreservedly to God, to surrender himself entirely to God's guiding Hand.

And thus the next section begins with the exact same words: "The Lord gave me . . ." "And the Lord gave me such faith in churches . . ." The period directly after his conversion when Francis still remained in the dark as far as his future was concerned, when he still did not know the will of God for him, now stands clearly before the eyes of his spirit in these last hours of his life as he lets his Testament be written.

It was in no way clear to him then how things would proceed for him. Only one thing was clear and certain within him: to let himself be led entirely by God, to do whatever the Lord gave him to do, to become disposable. Meantime he prayed earnestly for genuine faith, firm hope and perfect love, as he himself expressed it in the prayer after his conversion, and to recognize and accept what is right so that he could fulfill God's sacred mandate, even though he still did not know what it would be.

The Lord in return had compassion on his servant Francis engulfed in darkness. From the image of the Crucified in San Damiano he spoke these words of direction to him: "Francis, go rebuild my house which you see is completely falling to ruin." Again Francis received a very concrete mission just as with the leper whom God placed in his path. I almost want to say, a very insignificant mission. Had he been converted just to mend churches? Was that the meaning of these months of struggling, merely to repair churches? Francis did not question it. He had heard that he should rebuild the house of the Lord which was about to collapse. "He prepared himself to obey and gave himself completely to the fulfillment of this command," says Celano.

Francis left the world and repaired first of all the crumbling churches in the neighborhood of Assisi for he first understood these indicative words of God about his falling house to mean literally the little church of San Damiano and other such churches. During the protracted period of his conversion he had frequently prayed in these churches and yet up until now had hardly noticed their dilapidation because he was so used to it; he had found nothing amiss in it and therefore had not felt himself called upon to better it. Now the command from the Lord opened his eyes to "recognize and accept what is right" so that he was sensitive to the unseemly and planned to remedy the situation, even to giving himself up entirely to this work of repair. His eyes had learned to see what formerly went unnoticed, exactly as when, in responding to the impulse from God, he showed merciful love to the lepers. In the act of being obedient, Francis learned to see in a new way; through obeying he learned to recognize what God wanted. Once again he was changed, as Thomas of Celano gives witness: "Through and through he felt the inexpressible transformation of his being." Thus he remained open for God's further guidance.

Francis himself revealed to his brothers that the Holy Spirit had later taught him to understand the words of the Crucified about repairing the churches as referring to that Church which Christ had redeemed by his Blood. From the tangible churches of stone on which he worked, which he repaired and improved, Francis learned that great mystery of seeing the Church which Christ had redeemed through his holy Cross — the community of redeemed mankind. For this "so much faith" which God gave Francis "in churches," the comprehension of which so transformed his life, Francis gives thanks plainly and simply here in his Testament.

". . . that I prayed and said simply . . ." In saints prayer appears as the direct and first result of faith. Prayer, however, is faith lived; in prayer faith finds its expression. Prayer is the connecting link between faith and life, between faith and action. Lofty and exalted intellectual faith is worthless if it does not become a living action. Yet how can it become a living thing without prayer? Francis also experienced this. Thus, according to the witness of his biographers, he was a man "who did not trust in his own actions, but anticipated all matters with holy prayer." This experience, which is of such tremendous importance for all Christian living, he declares here again almost incidentally as though it were grossly self-evident.

Great faith, however, does not result in just prayer, but in the "prayer of simplicity." What does that mean? The more something pertains to the purely human realm, the more complicated it is. The more man trusts in himself, relying on his own wisdom and capability, the more circumstances and things become involved, the more entangled he becomes in his own world. So much becomes doubtful and ambiguous, scintillating and blurred, unimportant and insignificant because the central support, which God alone can be, is missing. However, the more man opens himself to the world of God in faith and submits himself in faith-filled readiness, the more simple everything becomes. The more man strikes roots in God's world through faith, looks to God in all things great and small, attempts to see all things from God's point of view, the more will complications fade. Wherever man trusts in God, lets himself be totally guided and directed by Him, there man, things and circumstances fall into their rightful place, namely, according to the order established by God. There everything becomes plain, clear and meaningful. What has been said applies above all to prayer. The less genuine faith there is, the more complicated, involved and trivial prayer becomes.

I had an aunt who was a Carmelite in the Carmel of Dachau. One could converse well with her about such things. One time we were talking about prayer and I said to her, "Basically, the older a person becomes, the more lucid and simple prayer be-

comes. When I think about my novitiate, one could become en-
raptured with his own prayer." Then she said to me, "It should
be so, because the closer one comes to God the simpler it is
since God is simplicity, God is lucid in himself." For this reason
we should not long for the enthusiasm and rapture of our novitiate
prayer.

I believe there is also a development toward simplicity, toward
simplifying, so that it becomes utterly plain and clear, as Francis
says, that, "pure lucid, holy simplicity confounds the wisdom of the
world and the wisdom of the flesh." Here ends all human pon-
dering and planning on our part; here one can only look to God
and his divine action and in this light pray, saying in all simplicity,
"We adore you, O Lord Jesus Christ — here and in all your
churches all over the world, and we bless you, because by your
holy cross you have redeemed the world." One almost wants to
say, "Is that all?" That is genuine prayer of simplicity. That is
prayer as an expression of that great faith in the Church which
Francis received as a precious gift from God.

Adoration and gratitude are the substance of this genuine but
plain and simple prayer which Francis taught his first brothers
to pray. And they prayed it bowing low, with their faces to the
earth, whenever they saw a church, even in the distance, or a
cross along the way. Francis adored the Lord Jesus Christ not
only in the church where he happened to find himself but in all
the churches in the whole world in which the Holy Mass was
celebrated, in which the Holy Eucharist was preserved. This great
mystery he learned by looking with faith: the mystery of the Lord
giving himself to us.

Francis' love for the lepers was but a reflection of this mystery
of the merciful love of God. Every self-surrender, every self-
sacrifice and every self-giving which, awakened by experience of
Divine Mercy who sacrificed himself for us, reveals and material-
izes itself as merciful love toward the suffering, and becomes
adoration, submission, "bending low to the earth" before the Lord
himself. Both sprout from the same root and only thus can it be
genuine: this mercy toward others and grateful adoration toward

God — to put it in modern terms: the horizontal and the vertical — which can never be separated from each other. Adoration of the Lord, which is not at the same time devotion to persons, loving service to the least and to the rejected — at the time of Francis, the lepers — such adoration is a play on words and an empty pretense; it remains within the walls of the church, God's House, but it never ventures forth into life. On the other hand, service of our neighbor which does not realize and embody adoration of the Lord, remains purely humanitarian, something from the realm of noble humanity where man himself decides whether he will show mercy or not.

"In all the churches of the world," here means nothing other than those places where genuine adoration of Christ immolated, carried out by an adoring people, must be demonstrated as genuine through merciful love for all men: for sinners and for those who do me nothing but wrong, those who are offensive and hateful to me; also toward those whom I would most prefer to avoid as Francis did the lepers. Whoever then has great faith in what happens daily among us in all the churches of the world adores the Lord in simplicity: that is, he gives of himself totally, claiming for himself only the right to be obedient to the will of God and to be completely an instrument of love in God's hand. Such a believer truly no longer knows a "double standard" but rather in all simplicity serves nothing but the Lord in all his members, regardless.

That this our interpretation is correct is shown us in the second part of the prayer: ". . . and we bless you because by your holy cross you have redeemed the world." Praising, blessing, in Latin, benedicere — this means speaking well of someone, praising, confirming goodness, thanking. One can also translate it as: We are glad and rejoice, we are grateful, Lord that through your holy cross you have saved the world. Thus Francis, in his tremendous faith and simple prayer offered thanks in all the churches for the grace of our redemption.

From the hour in which the Crucified spoke to him in the little church of San Damiano, according to the words of Celano, "his soul was pierced with 'compassio Crucifixi,' with compassion for Christ crucified." At that time "the stigmata of the venerable passion were deeply imprinted in his heart, though not as yet on his flesh." In this participation in the redemptive offering of Christ, the simple faith of Francis actually hit upon this essential point of mankind's salvation history. Here he found the work of God to which all is related and in the light of which everything must be seen. His living became a dying with Christ, "so that Christ crucified, whom he carried deep within his heart, was also visibly stamped upon his external life." He became, as Bonaventure so beautifully put it, the "bearer and servant of the Cross of Christ." Thus Francis offered thanks for the grace of redemption not only with the words of pious prayers — which are often not obligating and furthermore cost little — but with a gratitude which impelled him to fulfill in his own life the suffering of Christ even to sharing the suffering of the Crucified.

Francis not only blessed and praised the Lord who redeemed us through his cross, but he lived and proclaimed through his very life that which he previously as well as presently praised and blessed in prayer. And in so doing, his faith grew thruogh the grace of God. The Holy Spirit was able to lead him into deeper understanding of each word that the Crucified spoke to him at the beginning of his conversion. Francis learned to apply each "divine word to the Church which Christ had redeemed at the cost of his own Blood." The participation in the sufferings and death of Christ became for him his most important service in the building of the Church which was at that time so dangerously near collapse.

It appears to me, one might also say that in these first two paragraphs of his Testament, Francis — as simply as it may seem — actually describes here the decisive characteristics of his conversion. Thus God gave him a conversion from a worldly to a Christian life; thus his heart became transformed under the influence of grace; Francis learned to give freely and without measure God's love and mercy which he had received to overflowing and without limit. In return for God's merciful love which is boundlessly manifest in the cross of Christ, Francis learned to render adoration and praise gratefully — but not only in words, in pious hymns, in declarations of love within the walls of church buildings, but in imitation of Christ's life. In so doing he lost himself in his total abandonment to the service of the Church for which Christ had given Himself. Thus he became the living image of Christ of whom Pope Innocent III could say in anticipation: "That is truly the man through whose deeds and teachings the Church of Christ will be shored up." To support the Church of Christ through word and deed, through life and teaching, in imitation of St. Francis, is also the meaning of our religious life. To this has God called us; to this end will God increasingly transform us day by day, even convert us. For this should we totally abandon ourselves to Him as converts, as instruments.

Therefore it is important first of all that we keep ourselves ever open, as did Francis, to the providence and guidance of God; that we remain ever ready to accept his directions and to fulfill them in obedience.

It would be a mistake to act at any time as though we already know exactly wherein lies the goal of our conversion, where our service for the kingdom of God in building his Church must lie. We should never conclusively commit ourselves as if that which we consider right and ideal corresponds directly to God's will. Is there not often much egoism behind such lofty idealism — so-called idealism? Francis waited and prayed. He kept himself ready for anything that the Lord might give him. And when the Lord gave him something, he was ready to obey. For him, always and in all things, there was that decisive: "The Lord gave me . . ." And because he was ready to do whatever the Lord made known to him here and now as mandate, he learned to understand more comprehensively and more deeply the will of God by his doing it.

As Francis perceived the words of the Crucified, he did not say: Is this why I left the world, to do the work of a mason? No, he began in all humility to repair dilapidated churches although he could well have asked: Is that all there is? Is that really so important? Can the Lord value this so highly? Should I have left the world to repair chapels into which no one even goes anymore? Francis did not question in this way. He set to work and did first of all what lay at hand. But in working on the stone churches he came to recognize their mysterious reality as the place of the renewal of the redeeming act of Christ. The more he submitted himself to this reality, the more he experienced in the churches of stone the mystery of the living Church which begins anew each day to live and grow from the offering of Christ. At the same time he grew also in the real meaning of his life — to rebuild and support the living Church through offering and suffering with Christ. In active faith, which ever increased, he gave himself more and more to the Lord. Because he simply did what the Lord said, the love which enabled him to do all things grew.

This love also grew concretely evident, naturally speaking, even in the fetching and carrying of materials for building the churches, just as it grew in the concretely visible service which he bestowed on the lepers. Genuine love for persons — that becomes obvious to us here and we dare not overlook it — can never be purely spiritual. Love needs to give external evidence of its growth. Our love for God, for the Church, for mankind, must make itself actively felt, visible and experienced. Within the Church, in his practical concern for her, Francis received his great faith, the foundation of love. He received it because he prayed, because he prayed in simplicity as only faith in God and his salvation can make possible. In such prayer he overcame himself. He did not try through his prayer, and that is the prayer of simplicity, to make God the servant of man as is so often the intent of our prayer. He did not try, as we so often do, to influence God, begging him so that He will finally give in to do our will. No, Francis overcame himself; he adored, he thanked, he praised, the great mercy of God in his Son. Adoring and thanking, he lost himself, giving himself up completely to the redeeming work of the Lord. His conversion was so complete that he penetrated the redeeming love of Christ who saved the Church through his own Blood.

Is it not true that we must likewise be more open to the guiding and directing hand of God? Prepared to let our life be determined entirely by him? Must we not begin more simply to do here and now what is revealed to us precisely in this here-and-now moment as God's will? Must we not be pliant instruments in his Hand, under his guidance now in order to recognize more and more what we must do later? Must we not relinquish our playing around with grandiose ideas and lofty, exalted plans, in order to carry out for once in simplicity the purely practical, to perform the lesser and least tasks which through persons, things and situations God brings into our path of life right in this moment as opportunity for a service of love? Must we not accomplish all this first of all prayerfully, adoringly, gratefully? In prayer we shall experience God's love and whoever truly loves can truly devote himself entirely to God's work. And whoever gives himself entirely to God's saving work will be capable of loving Him even more because he has overcome himself, he has let himself be forgotten precisely because he has been truly converted; he lives totally aligned with God.

Through conversion of heart the purpose of our Franciscan religious life reveals itself more and more: to live in penance, to live totally turned toward God, to whatever the Lord gives us to do, so that we too can say:

"The Lord gave to me, and then I did what He gave me to do."

IV

GOD'S GIFTS AND MANDATES
(Section 3)

In the initial statement of his Testament Francis, as a person converted, looked back gratefully on the work of the Lord who led him to conversion so that his life became a life of penance. If we look at the separate incidents, then we notice how Francis stressed in gratitude each moment when, through God's love, his life became a response to love. First of all there was the encounter with the leper in merciful love whereby Francis learned to forget himself in order to give his total love to Christ in this suffering person, a love which formerly had been centered in and before all else on himself. Then there was the confrontation with the person of Christ in churches. This gifted him with faith in *the* Church where Christ's redemption resided and in which thereafter he always and everywhere returned thanks for this redemption. In both encounters Francis learned to submit to what God ordained and found love through obedience to the provident Hand of God. He accepted without reserve what the Lord sent Him; above all, he accepted everything gratefully and made a return of all to the Lord, for God's gifts were commands to be complied with by his actions, by his whole existence.

In the third point of his Testament, of which we today will consider only the first part, Francis continues to speak with simple gratitude of God's gifts which he regards as mandates whose carrying out further accomplished and perfected his conversion. There he says:

"Then the Lord gave me, and gives me now, towards priests who live according to the law of the Holy Roman Church, so great a confidence, by reason of their priesthood, that even if they sought to persecute me, I would nonetheless return to them. And if I were to have as great a wisdom as Solomon possessed, and were to meet with poor priests of this world, I do not wish to preach without their consent in the parishes in which they dwell. And these and all others I wish to reverence, love and honor as my lords. And I do not wish to discover if they are sinners, because I behold in them the Son of God, and they are my lords. And for this reason I do this: because in this world I see nothing with my bodily eyes of Him who is the most high Son of God except His most holy Body and His most holy Blood, which they receive and which they alone minister to others."

Let us proceed point by point. "Then the Lord gave me, and gives me now, towards priests who live according to the law of the Holy Roman Church, so great a confidence, by reason of their priesthood, that even if they sought to persecute me, I would nonetheless return to them." Here it is again made clear what we already noticed in the very first section: persons turned totally toward God have a completely different outlook.

Francis did not judge persons and things according to the measure and standard ordinarily used by others. This is an important point to remember, that persons converted to Christ no longer see people and things with purely human eyes, but rather with the eyes of God. Thus, to Francis lepers were no longer persons to be shunned, but instead Christ his brother whom he could serve in merciful love. Thus, to him churches were no longer merely stone buildings, but instead an image of *the* Church which exists thanks to Christ's sacrifice on the cross and which constantly leads people to a precious gratitude. Thus also to the converted Francis priests of this Church were no longer seen as persons like the rest of us, but as something more and this "by reason of their priesthood." Francis specifically stressed this point, that for no other reason — neither charismatic gifts nor greater intelligence nor stronger character — were they chosen from among the multitude of the faithful. Because of their Orders they have become God's special instruments whom God so uses that they become his representatives, so much so that in all difficulties a person can have recourse to them who represent Him, as Francis here states.

Again we see how concrete is the new faith-life which God granted Francis at his conversion, and how genuinely human it is. The merciful God, who is our refuge, has designated persons through whom we can find Him. He designated them through the sacrament of Orders by which they are mandated to carry on God's work of salvation among men. "As often as you do this, you do it in memory of Me." "Whose sins you forgive, they are forgiven them; whose sins you retain, they are retained." "Who hears you, hears Me; who rejects you, rejects Me. He, however, who rejects Me, rejects also Him who sent Me. Whoever accepts you, accepts Me; and whoever accepts Me, accepts also Him who sent Me." All these words of the Lord in the Gospel form the basis for Francis' faith, for his trust and loyal submission to priests. Through these words of Christ Himself is Francis' faith, his trust and his submission justified. Because the Lord unites himself in a special way to priests through their Orders, and in finding Him we find God the Father, we can have recourse to the priests of the Church, confidently returning to them in all our difficulties.

Naturally such a faith-filled attitude will be easy when we find priests who live completely according to the divine mission given them by their ordinatoin. It would then be cause for joy, and such an encounter with a God-filled, Spirit-filled person would strengthen and confirm our belief in God's merciful love. We need only think of Pope John XXIII. — This attitude of belief, however, can be very difficult, can even seriously be endangered, if we find priests who are not a genuine refuge but rather the opposite. Francis was aware of this difficulty; he had himself already experienced it. He had often enough in his life experienced that with priests, bishops, Cardinals it could be otherwise. But because he saw in priests, by reason of their Orders — let it once more be clearly stated, not because of their personal attributes — the representatives, the guardians of God's love, he will, as he here specifically says, return to those priests even if they should persecute him.

Who cannot feel here the deep faith of the person of Francis. Humanly speaking, one might be shocked by this deep faith-view which actually runs counter to people's natural sentiments. One might be even more shocked that Francis speaks of this so simply as though there were no problem, as if it were the most obvious thing in the world. Yes, it is obvious to persons who accept God's gift of priests, who accept from God this faith, this trust, this sincerity — and therefore Francis began by stressing "the Lord gave me and gives me . . ." Doesn't that sound like jubilant gratitude?

But the practice, the living experience of Francis went even further and therefore here in his Testament, looking back, he goes one decisive step further still. He knows that the conflict between faith and life can be even greater here, namely, when a person extraordinarily gifted by God — a charismatic, as we like to say today — encounters a priest who really is not what he should be. Francis here solves this conflict situation by citing a very pointed example through which he reveals his own attitude.

"And if I were to have as great a wisdom as Solomon possessed, and were to meet with poor priests of this world, I do not wish to preach without their consent in the parishes in which they dwell."

If God had given me, Francis would here say, as great a wisdom as He in His grace gave the Old Testament King Solomon, — that absolutely wise man, he who was the wisest person of his time and was unquestionably regarded as such also by the Middle Ages — if I also, Francis would say, were so highly blessed by God, even then I would not use this gift of grace in the Church against the wishes of the person officially appointed by God, against the wishes of the duly authorized priest. Yes, he would subordinate this charism, this great gift of grace even to such priests as were sinful, wretched and slaves of this world. He would even go so far as to make his service in the Church dependent upon their consent. Here each of us would ask: why? Why this attitude? Francis knew, and this section confirms it, the objective which is grounded in the ordination of priests in the Church, which is independent also of their personal failures. Francis knew the mandate given the priest by God and submitted himself to them even with his extraordinary gifts of. grace.

This, his obedient subordination, is not, however, the ultimate. Francis would do still more and that is, he would show respect for these poor priests of the world and for all others, would love them and honor them as "my lords." Shocked, we would again query: these sinners? These persons enslaved by the world; these men who so often hinder goodness? These he will love and honor? To these he will render respect as to his lords? No, not to these men; rather to these priests who represent the Lord, in whom the believing Francis comes into close contact with God, in whom he encounters the Lord God. To these priests, he emphasizes this, he renders honor because of their ordination and for no other reason. Because of their consecration, he loves them; through Orders they have become his masters. This is because in ordination Christ has incorporated Himself in them in a special way so that they are capable of acting in His Name and in His stead. This "being Christ" of the priest is a grace from God which does not affect the humanity of those who receive this grace as an unearned gift from God. This "being" cannot be destroyed in any way. Francis says this again in his firm childlike faith and with inimitable simplicity: "And I do not wish to discover if they are sinners, because I behold in them the Son of God, and they are my lords."

We see how Francis looked beyond external appearances and gazed at the graced reality. The priest is for him a manifestation of Christ the Son of God; is to him a concrete, visible image of

Christ, even if and when he is a sinner. Here we sense ultimate faith. In this believing gaze, which he expresses as so self-evidently simple, Francis reveals himself again as the person directed totally toward God, as a person detached from self, from his own purely human manner of considering things and who is thus centered in the world of God in which he quite obviously and naturally lived. Here what is so complicated and often miserably difficult from a human standpoint, is looked at from God's viewpoint, is seen in simple faith and more properly matches the reality.

Perhaps as Francis thought about his Brothers he felt something of the boldness of which he had here so simply spoken. Would they all understand it; would they all grasp it? For them, therefore, he added a reason, a basis which for him at this point of his life was precious and to which he turned again and again.

"And for this reason I do this: because in this world I see nothing with my bodily eyes of Him who is the most high Son of God except His most holy Body and His most holy Blood, which they receive and which they alone minister to others."

With these words Francis not only firmly grounds his faith in the value of the priesthood but also gives expression of his gratitude that it is the priest who dispenses life to him. It is truly the priest and he alone who is the authorized minister of the central mystery of Christian faith and then of Christian life. Certainly he alone is the minister of the Eucharist. Through the sacrament of Orders he was given the power to re-present the saving act of Christ so that all the faithful could partake of and participate in it. By reason of the powers conveyed upon them to change bread and wine into the most holy Body and most precious Blood of the most high Son of God, they make possible our participation and our integration into Christ's redeeming sacrifice on the cross, for which Francis, as he said in the preceding statement, wished to give thanks in all the churches of the world when he prayed the "Adoremus te." Priests enable us to come close to Christ, the Son of God, allow us to look upon Him in this mystery. We thank Him for this when we are allowed to encounter Christ over and over again in our life.

For this reason, and we must emphasize this once again, only for this reason, did Francis render priests honor; for this reason he loved them; for this reason he respected them as his lords — and therefore he did not look upon their sinfulness. For this reason he did not let himself be misled in his faith when he had to admit that even priests are poor miserable creatures. Gratefully he accepted from them the gifts which they receive directly from the Hand of God and offer to God in man's stead without God's gift being affected by their human frailties.

Thomas of Celano recounts in his *First Life of St. Francis* that the first Brothers preferably, as he says, and with a special humility went to confession to a priest in Assisi who had a bad reputation. Precisely in those times when so many pious Christians were in error regarding the Church and the priesthood in the Church, believing that it was the "charism" and not ordination which was crucial, Francis and his Brothers continually lived according to the belief that whatever God grants, through whatever instrument, was truly granted and not bound by the limitations of the instrument. Francis, the man of faith, stressed this once again in his Testament before he departed from this world. This faith which the Lord gave him in the priesthood within the Church he wished to bequeath in his Testament to all his future children as a precious inheritance.

If we have been able to gain valuable and helpful insights into the deep faith-life of Francis from the first two parts of his Testament, we can look even deeper in this third point into his unquestionably freeing faith, contrary to all human manner of thinking. Whoever seeks to penetrate deeper and deeper into these simple and unpretentious words of the Testament will be astounded and impressed by the conversion wonder which God's grace effected in Francis. Then may the longing be awakened in us that we, lowly weak followers of Father Francis, might also be granted conversion to such a life of faith. And whoever will deny that precisely this concrete faith of Francis is necessary in the Church of God today, let him.

In addition, it should first of all be noted that Francis saw all

the steps of his conversion as gifts from God. The Lord gave it
to him. God's gifts, however, must be asked for, just as Francis
prayed earnestly in solitary places at the beginning of his conversion. He prayed for complete surrender, as his biographer tells
us, so that the eternal and true God might direct him in His Way
and teach him to do His Will. Francis endured great anguish of
soul and found no rest until he fulfilled in reality what he had
accepted in his heart. Perhaps Francis had preferred to ask for
other things for himself; he had dreamed of other things. God's
Way for him was different. The Will of God for him was different.
And Francis prayed with great spiritual torment until he reached
the point of following God's Way and of doing God's Will.

Such prayer must also find its place in our lives. Let us often
ask ourselves: do we, in our prayer, attempt to make God docile
to us — to get Him "on our side" so that He does what we want
instead of our being "on His side" in order to follow His Way
and do His Will? In our prayer and in our corresponding living
there must be that readiness which leaves us no rest until we have
fulfilled what God has given us to do, what we have received in
grace and as gift in our hearts. God grants us faith and gives us
also the strength to live according to that faith. He especially gives
us the example and words of our Father Francis for this life lived
out of faith. It is up to us to put these gifts of God into operation
and to open ourselves to all mankind, particularly to those called
by Him as priests within the Church. They are the ones through
whom the Word of Life and the Bread of Life is dispensed. This
is not because they have any special human qualifications, but
rather because through the sacrament of Orders they are empowered and authorized by God; they have God's authority. This,
however, brings us to a primary difficulty which creates an obstacle to the actualization of our faith.

We are all aware of the fact that there is today a crisis of
authority just as there was in the time of Francis, although based
on other assumptions. Francis submitted himself to others because God gave these persons office, mission and power. He did
not look at the character of the instrument, but in genuine faith,

looked to the Hand of God who can and does give His grace, precisely as I say it, as He wills. How much then does this also apply to us — thus to be converted. We must turn ourselves about from a purely human point of view to a genuine faith point of view. It is not for us to give God the directions as to how and through whom He should lead and guide us, bless and animate us. We must humbly and gratefully see the generous Hand of God in all things which He gives us through the men He has empowered. Then we will render them respect. We will love and honor them as our masters because it is through them that God, the Lord, intervenes in our life and influences it.

This difficulty with authority becomes even greater when God has given us keener insight, sharper intelligence and greater wisdom than those who are his representatives to us and if we, as, for example, the preaching Francis with his greater charismatic blessing, could serve the Kingdom of God and its concerns better than they. Then submission in faith is definitely much more difficult. This means to submit my charismatic gifts and insights to the will of the person in office as to my master. This will testify that for us they stand in God's stead.

What Francis here teaches us is definitely the essence of the spirit of the Gospel and nothing can explain it better than the meeting of the Lord with the man born blind. The man wanted to see. What did the Lord do? He spat in the dust of the road, made a paste which He spread over the man's eyes and sent him to the Pool of Siloe saying: Wash there. The man could have said, "He needed only to touch me; why this roundabout way through the dust of the streets?" Here the evangelist adds an interesting observation: "He sent him to the Pool of Siloe, (a name that means 'sent') ," Jn 9:7, because they believed the healing waters of this pool were sent by God. Certainly Christ could have healed the man with one word as He had the blind men of Jericho. But He shows us here that He is not dependent upon the conceptions men make for themselves. Had the man persisted in his own judgment and had he not gone, he would have remained blind. Thus it was that because of some dust from the street and because of his faith his eyes were opened and he was able to see. And he adored Christ as the One sent by God. We notice here the same faith that we encounter with Francis. Moreover, we notice that such faith has a transforming effect also in our lives. Much is changed, becomes so very different, from that which is commonly accepted among men and from a purely human viewpoint. Furthermore, this total change is an important step toward our complete conversion. Whoever will risk this total change out of deep faith, will stride right out of the world of man, out of this all-too-human world, into the world of God. His life will become plain, simple and uncomplicated — of that the life of our Father Francis guarantees us. Why? Because in this attitude of belief man sees everything as coming from God and can accept everything out of His Hand, regardless through whom God gives it. "Then the Lord gave me, and gives me now, . . . so great a confidence . . ." Let us pray for this faith and try our best to make it a reality.

Let us join our holy Father Francis in praying:

> Most holy and glorious God,
> enlighten the darkness of my heart
> and grant me genuine faith,
> firm hope, and perfect love.
> Give me, O Lord,
> true perception and understanding,
> so that I may fulfill the holy mandate
> which in truth has been given me by You.

V

SOURCE OF LIVING FAITH
(Section 3 con'd)

Today we will consider the second half of part three of the Testament of St. Francis. There Francis says:

"And these most holy mysteries above all else I desire to be honored and adored and kept in precious places. Whenever I shall find writings with His most holy names and words in unbecoming places, I wish to gather them up and I ask that they be gathered up and laid in a more worthy place. And all theologians and those who impart the most holy words of God, we must honor and reverence as those who minister to us spirit and life."

The Testament of Francis, as we have seen and will further see, is a unique witness of Francis' attitude toward poverty. In this document he carries out what he himself exhorts others to do in his 19th Admonition: "Blessed is the servant who returns all the goods he has to the Lord God." In actuality, in his Testament he restores all goods at the close of his earthly life in utter gratitude to God, the Donor, and therefore the Lord and Owner. "The Lord has given me . . . The Lord Himself led me among the lepers . . . The Lord granted me . . . The Lord gave to me and gives me now . . . The Most High Himself revealed to me . . ." No one should add anything from the saints to what he had written, he says, because it was the Lord Himself who had worked through him. Thus the Testament becomes an avowal by the Poor Man of Assisi that he realized everything was given him by God in every instance.

The Testament is at the same time a witness of the unfathomable gratitude of this Poor Man who can do nothing but give back to God what belonged to God all along. As we have seen, Francis thanks God above all for:

— the gift and grace of faith which the Lord so obviously gave him;

— the gift and grace of faith in the Church;

— the gift and grace of faith in the priests of this Church, in whom he saw Christ Himself and whom he respected because they alone administer the mystery of the Holy Eucharist.

Thus the key word, so to speak, found in the continuation of the third point of the Testament is already indicated. Francis speaks of the source of his faith, or more precisely, of the source of his life of faith. For, as we notice here line by line, to Francis faith is not advanced knowledge but rather doing and living. To him it is a matter of living out the faith given him by God. This is what he speaks about in his Testament. Faith in a church of stone he had repaired led him to simple prayer and provided him with the clue to understanding the mystery of the Church which grew out of the redeeming suffering of Christ. This was the object of his gratitude in part two.

Confidence in the priests of the Church led him to return to them repeatedly even if they rejected him. This confidence led him to a respectful love and regard which gave him the clue to understanding the mystery of their mission — that Christ works through them even if they themselves are sinners. The reverence and loving esteem which he thus had for priests led him further to understand the mystery of the Eucharist through which Christ as Redeemer is again and again brought into the reality of our life. His faith in the great mysteries of God grew out of his carrying out in practice and acting in accord with what he believed. That is the deepest meaning of this grateful acknowledgment.

I believe the Franciscan School of the Middle Ages (St. Bonaventure and others) had grasped this very well. They all stressed that theology is a practical science, as Bonaventure said, so that we may be good Christians. We often study just to acquire knowledge, while the great Masters of the past always said that knowledge which does not act is dead. Man experiences reality in what he does, not in what he knows, which is only one side. That is surely an endowment from the heritage of St. Francis which we meet here in the Testament. It is precisely from this living faith, brought to actuality and made a reality in action, that is spoken of in this third section.

Francis, as has already been noted, thankfully mentions the source of his life lived out of faith: the mystery of the Eucharist, the Word of God, and the persons who are called to proclaim the word of God. (It can also be noted that we can parallel point by point texts from the introduction to the New Missal which are to be observed by the whole Church today, with what Francis had already expressed in the 13th century!) This holy mystery is Christ's sacred Body and his precious Blood which priests receive and which they alone administer to others. Here Francis does not say anything more about the content of this sacred mystery which is so central to his life of faith; it is sufficient for him to refer to the fact that he looks upon it as the most high Son of God, the Savior of all men. What really matters to him is that this Mystery must be revered above all, must be adored and preserved in precious places (all actions), by all of his followers for whom he is leaving this Testament.

Again Francis is concerned about the actions which must bear out the inner faith, the actions which must witness to and actualize the believing. We know from history, and especially from Francis' letter to all the clergy, that at that time much in this regard was in a sad state. The Eucharist was treated as a thing in spite of faith in the presence of Christ. There was truly a great lack of respect. Pope Honorius III had undertaken what amounted to an encyclical crusade to all the bishops of the Church exposing the grievous situations which existed. This definitely had an influence on Francis' letter to all the clergy and on his Testament.

Because Francis, in his great faith, here perceived the "most high Son of God Himself," he wished that the reverence due to Christ the Lord in his majesty should also be shown Him in this mystery. In the presence of the mystery of the Body of the Lord, every fiber of his being was ardently aglow. Here he gave the Lord ever anew the response to love by revering Him above all else. "Honored and adored" — what is ultimately meant by this veneration may be clarified by a word from Brother Thomas of Celano where he says of Francis: "Showing toward that Sacrament deserving of all reverence all the reverence he could, he offered a sacrifice of all his members, and receiving the Lamb that was offered, he immolated his own spirit with the fire that burned always upon the altar of his heart" (2C 201). For Francis adoration was not something external but rather the continual offering of oneself. He offered himself in his daily living in the same manner as he offered himself during the Eucharistic celebration. This is the adoration which he also expects of his followers. We can again see very clearly that our holy Father Francis was concerned with faith that was lived, which in this instance meant the perfect offering of the total person.

As to the third point, ". . . and kept in precious places": interior reverence, personal faith, can sustain itself only when it finds a suitable external expression. The person, as a body-soul being, requires to a certain extent, that all that is present in the spirit life of the soul must become visible and noticeable also for the body. The greatest reverence, which is respectful love and perfect adoration, shall then, as Francis expresses it, be made evident by preserving the Sacred Mysteries in precious places. The word "preciosa" is actually used. Here poverty must draw back where the Lord Himself is concerned. And for this reason he wished, as Celano recounts, "to send his brothers throughout the world with precious pyxes so that wherever they should see the price of our redemption kept in an unbecoming manner, they should place It in the very best place" (2C 201). And St. Clare, even though on her sickbed, prepared over 50 corporals (whoever has been in San Damiano in Assisi has seen them), enclosed them in silk or scarlet burses and consigned them to the various churches in the mountains and valleys around Assisi. It must be remembered that at that time there were no tabernacles; they came later. At most, the Eucharist was preserved in a dove-shaped container which hung above the altar, but ordinarily It lay in a niche to the side of the altar. Thus we see both saints were concerned that the "price of our redemption" as Thomas of Celano pointedly refers to It, should be preserved in precious surroundings. Through this concern for the externals the reverence which was customary during the celebration of the Sacred Mysteries was extended and completed.

In this concern for sacred vessels and for what remains after the consecration in the Mass, the reality, as Francis writes in his letter to the General Chapter, will be a lived reality. There he actually says, and I believe we should think more about this today in connection with so many experiments, "the better to impress on us the majesty of our Creator and our subjection to him," we should see these external signs not merely as external accidentals — obviously they can be simply that, that's clear — but they should rather always be the external expression of their inner meaning. Then the external and internal will mutually penetrate and benefit each other. The little things of everyday living let the greater things become an experienced reality, an experienced reality for the total person, for body and soul.

The love of Francis for the Blessed Sacrament and his reverence for this Sacred Mystery draws forth again and again his parallel reverent love for the Word of God. This is also surprising: what we have considered as something tremendously new from the Council (Vatican II) — "the table of the Word and the table of the Sacred Bread," "the liturgy of the Word and the liturgy of the Eucharist," — we find was always intimately bound together by Francis. He never speaks of one without the other. For him both exist in close relationship, intimately bound together, as the

Council expects them to be. Here in the Testament we find it again.

If we ask the reason for this, we can find the desired explanation and the basic reasons in the Letter to the General Chapter. "So I admonish all my Brothers and encourage them in Christ" — one can see already by the elaborate introduction how important this was to Francis — "that wherever they find any of the written words of God, they should give them all the reverence they can, and if the words are not well put away or lie strewn about improperly anywhere, they should gather them up and put them away as far as they may do so," — then comes the reason: "honoring in the words the Lord who has spoken" This is very simply stated; the Council expressed it more theologically, but Francis had the same attitude. Because the Lord is living here in his Word, we wish to honor Him by preserving his Word, the written Word, with all due respect: "honoring in the words the Lord who has spoken." Francis obviously recognized the twofold presence of Christ of which the Constitution on the Liturgy and the post-Conciliar documents speak so clearly today, i.e., Christ present to us in the Sacrament of the Altar and in his Word. This is why Francis worshiped the Lord in the Blessed Sacrament and this is why he worshiped the Lord in his Word. Here the deep faith of Francis becomes apparent: he knew Christ spoke to him directly in the Word of God, in the words of Sacred Scripture.

We are all familiar with the words which Francis said to the first two who joined him: "Let us go early in the morning to the church and taking the book of the Gospel, let us seek counsel from Christ" (2C 15). Francis went with the two to the Gospel as one goes to a master, as to Christ personally, so that they might be advised by Him. Great faith is here again made concrete through small things. Francis could not tolerate it if personal indifference for the Word of God was boasted of or led to irreverent treatment. "Whenever," says Thomas of Celano, "he would find anything written, whether about God or about man, along the way, or in a house, or on the floor, he would pick it up with the greatest reverence and put it in a sacred or decent place, so that the name of the Lord would not remain there or anything else pertaining to it" (1C 82). And this Francis also asked his followers to do in his Testament shortly before his death. It must have been a cause of great concern to him.

Then in a third place Francis also met his Lord; from a third source his faith received nourishment and life — from theologians and those who preach the holy word of God. Francis obviously had already learned that faith comes from hearing, as St. Paul says. Therefore he listened to the teachers of theology and to the preachers because by their office they were the servants of faith. "Sacred" he called their office, and all those who administered it, worthy of esteem. "They are," he says, "the life of the body; they, the warriors against the evil spirit; they, the light of the world." And as he once was writing to St. Anthony who was well versed in theology, he began the letter with the words, "To Brother Anthony, my Bishop." What the bishop was for the local church — the guardian of the word of God through which Christ the Lord speaks and works — that the theologians, the doctors of divinity, were to Francis: those who dispensed spirit and life through God's word. Francis regarded them therefore with utmost esteem and respectful deference. Everything to the contrary that was said hundreds of years later about Francis' opposition to theology and to study is rendered fictional by these simple words. To this belong first of all those certain groups within the Order who believed themselves to be the "Order of the future" and of whom Abbot Joachim of Fiore long ago spoke as the "Order in the era of the Holy Spirit" where one need study no longer but where each would be directly enlightened by the Holy Spirit. — Well, that era has not yet arrived, so we should calmly continue to study as St. Francis intended.

If we can now look back over these first three paragraphs of the Testament, perhaps we can summarize them as follows: Francis recalled in gratitude the meetings with his Lord Jesus Christ and the variety of ways in which he encountered Him. He met Christ:

— *in the lepers* toward whom he showed merciful love. He met Christ and became a changed person, a person who lived Gospel penance. He met Christ

— *in the churches* in which he prayed in simplicity. He met Christ and overflowed with prayerful gratitude for the grace of our redemption. He met Him

— *in the priests of the Church* toward whom he was filled with complete trust and loving esteem. He met them and looked upon Christ the most high Son of God Himself in them. He met Christ in a loving manner, as he himself says,

— *in the mystery of the Eucharist* in which he rendered all due reverence, adoration and love to the Sacred Presence. He met Christ and became a person who sacrificed and offered himself, perfecting ever more and more his conversion. He met the Lord

— *in his Word* which he heard and accepted in faith. He met Him and became more and more permeated with the life and light of Christ. Finally, he met the Lord

— *in the theologians and preachers* who present the most holy word of God to us and thus are mediators between God and us. He met Christ and received in this encounter spirit and life.

Thus the first part of the Testament becomes a hymn of gratitude for all the encounters with the Lord which the Lord himself gave and gives.

The value of this thanksgiving hymn is also in its witness of the direct personal contact of Francis with Christ the Lord. We notice this sentence after sentence. Christ is not for him someone enthroned in another world in unending unapproachable majesty who benevolently accepts the service of his menials as pictured in the old basilicas. Christ was not situated somewhere and somehow in Francis' life so that He was just occasionally seen and noticed. No, Christ was a real Presence central in the life of this saint; He was directly accessible. (ere we can recall Art. 7 of the Constitution on the Liturgy from the Council documents.) Francis met Christ in multiple ways; always and everywhere he encountered the truly credible Christ, the living and enduring Christ-among-us. Francis is not a credulous know-it-all but rather one who lived out his believing, dealing in faith with Christ. He truly had direct personal contact with Christ.

At this point I think we should at least consider whether or not much has become too restricted for us. We are familiar with practically only one manner of Christ's presence; and when we are not right in the church, we are far away from Him, we have nothing to do with Him. Always and everywhere Francis had something to do with Christ. In all his daily living he encountered the mysteriously present Christ. That was definitely one of the greatest graces in the life of St. Francis, his special charism.

Who among us would not also wish to share in this grace? It would also be for us, for our Franciscan religious life, the greatest grace; such a grace, however, one cannot force. Let us recall once again: "The Lord gave me . . . The Lord led me . . . Then the Lord gave me and gives me now . . ." Here God is the giver, and man must ask. "Ask and you shall receive — for whoever asks, receives; whoever seeks, finds." "How much more will your Father in heaven give the Holy Spirit to those who ask Him." The Lord cannot show us the way any clearer in the Gospel than with these words of his. "Whoever has ears to hear, let him hear!"

We must beg for God's grace; we must also thank Him for it. Only those who are grateful will preserve God's grace as a precious gift, just as Francis did in his Testament, by giving to God what is God's. God's giving to us must always be matched by our returning to Him, a return in full gratitude. Then can God's action be perfected in co-operative action. The return in total gratitude is not accomplished just in words, in some prayers, in hymns, but rather in all the deeds of life. Our whole life, down to the smallest point, must be a genuine reality of gratitude. Precisely here it must be stressed "even in the minutiae of daily life." Then it will match the teaching of St. Francis in his Testament.

— Whoever is truly grateful for the grace-laden *presence of Christ in all baptized persons* will show merciful love to each person and love each one, even the disagreeable, the suffering, the repulsive fellowman — let us say it, even to those so loathsome as the lepers were. And especially to these!

— Whoever is truly grateful for the *priesthood within the Church* through which Christ the Lord becomes redeemingly visible for us, will love and respect priests as his lords and not pay attention to their sins because he sees the Son of God in them.

(As I was preparing this conference yesterday, I asked myself a question about the internal relationship of the third paragraph: Why did Francis knowingly mention faith in priests, in contrast to the charismatics of his time, before he spoke of the sources of his Christian life, the Eucharist, the word of God and the preachers of God's word? Because he considered the sources reserved for Christ. They must be independent of every purely human claim. Christ worked in them; we encounter Christ in them; Christ intervenes in our lives through them, regardless of the external appearances of these instruments which he happens to use. It is exactly this teaching which Francis here imparts to us that seems so important to me for today — "and I do not wish to discover if they are sinners." He respected priests because he saw the Son of God working in and through them.)

— Whoever is grateful for the *great mystery of the Eucharist* finds it self-evident, and will do everything possible, that this most holy mystery is everywhere revered, adored and preserved in precious surroundings. No effort will be too great, and even the smallest details will be looked to.

— Whoever is grateful for the *presence of Christ in his Word,* a gift to us, will furnish the Sacred Scriptures with a special place of honor. Surely, it is a nuisance each time that I need the Scriptures to have to get up and go to it, to have to take the Book from its place of honor in order to use it. But this is a reminder each time that I am not taking just any book, but the Book of books. Having to stand up and go to the Bible makes it clear that here something different is being done than when I just reach behind me and take a book off the shelf. Let's not think that this is a small thing. Man is not a spirit being but a body-soul being and therefore this pertains to him. Therefore we should take the Sacred Scriptures in

hand with utmost respect and all due reverence.
— Then we will also meet in gratitude and respect *those men who give us God's word and through it administer spirit and life to us.*

I believe we can conclude by saying that precisely this actualized gratitude will preserve us from ever being indifferent or uncaring. Whoever is thus thankful, remains alert and watchful for the encounter with the living Christ in our midst. To him, as to our holy Father Francis, Christ will be the Living Center of his life — He with whom he always and everywhere has direct personal contact —

— in person-to-person encounters
— in the Church
— in his ministers
— in the sacraments
— in his Word.

He is always confronted with the reality of Christ who came to redeem and to sanctify our lives from within.

> O God,
> You have given us the blessing
> of our holy Father Francis
> as teacher and guide
> in our following of your only-begotten Son;
> grant to us
> who seek to follow him
> the grace of sharing in his glory in heaven.
> Through Christ our Lord. Amen.

VI

GRATEFUL RESPONSE
(Section 4)

We now turn our attention to the fourth paragraph of the Testament of our holy Father St. Francis, to that section in which he takes up again the historical account begun in the first paragraph.

"And after the Lord had given me brethren, no one showed me what I was to do, but the most High himself revealed to me that I should live according to the pattern of the holy Gospel. And I caused it to be written in few words and simple manner, and the Lord Pope confirmed it to me. And those who came to us to accept this way of life gave to the poor whatever they might have had. And they were content with one habit, quilted inside and out (if they wished), and with a cord and breeches. And we had no desire for aught else. The clerics among us prayed the Office like other clerics, while the laics said the Our Father. And quite willingly we would live in the (poor and abandoned) churches. And we were (simple and) without learning, and subject to all."

In the first paragraph of his Testament, Francis gratefully acknowledged how the Lord converted him interiorly and led him

123

to a totally Christian life. Gratefully he acknowledged that God, through his grace, had preserved him first and foremost from slipping into heresy. Filled with gratitude, he referred to the sources which continually nourished his Christian life, his life in God. To be sure, the word "thanksgiving" is not used even once. Therefore we should here pose the question: "Have we read too much into it? Were our conclusions forced?" I don't believe so, because this is precisely the greatness of Francis' way:

He does not merely say thanks — he is thanks!

Francis' entire attitude of thankfulness out of which he writes his Testament is revealed line after line. He claims nothing in his life for himself; he reckons nothing to his own credit; he attributes nothing to his own action. Everything in his life is the work of God; everything is God's grace. Everything is a gift given him by God. All that the poor Francis admits in utter simplicity will be spoken of in the Testament in genuine plainness; his gratitude will in all simplicity become a hymn of thanks to God, to the Lord who had worked such marvels in the life of his servant Francis and who continues to work in him. The self-forgetfulness of the totally Poor One who keeps nothing of himself back for himself but rather in all things gives to God what is God's, or better said, gives back to God what is God's own — this self-forgetfulness, a living interior poverty, is at the same time and in itself the highest gratitude and therefore true glorification of God.

We witness this same attitude in the fourth paragraph of the Testament where Francis looks back in utter thankfulness to the beginning of his fraternity, to the beginnings of the Order of Friars Minor. His words become even more plain, his speech more unadorned, the train of thought more simple as Francis now describes how the Order came into existence — this Order which already in 1226, even as Francis is drawing up his Testament, had entered all the countries of Christendom, whose members numbered in the thousands, this Order which had grown from a tiny seedling into a great tree spreading wide its branches to men of all nations, all levels of society and offered admission to every race.

Francis could have truly looked with holy pride at this astounding work. But no; the greater the work became, the smaller he made himself in order to be but an instrument in the Hand of God — herein he also remained true to his Lady Poverty. He remained ever the Little Poor Man saying: *"And after the Lord had given me brethren."* Is the fact that men came to him to live together with him not due, as history teaches, to the fact that Francis kindled a spark in them by his example? Did he not win them by his life of penance, by his radical self-giving to God? And yet Francis steps completely into the background, gratefully acknowledging that "the Lord had given me brethren."

Francis had, as we know with certainty today, a clarity of vision and full awareness of his times. He knew exactly the distress of the kingdom of God. He knew also the means of saving it. He and his brothers entered into many of the churches of that time and into the history of salvation, but here again Francis steps completely into the shadows: *"The most High himself revealed to me that I should live according to the pattern of the holy Gospel."* Certainly these words of humble gratitude also have the ring of duty-bound constancy.

Francis knew he was called directly by God: *"No one showed me what I was to do."* God's summons had come to him directly without human intervention having played a hand in it. This consciousness of mission carried Francis through all the difficulties of his lifetime. His whole life was a thank-filled response to this call from God which led him into the life of the Lesser Brothers. With restless but unwavering loyalty Francis gave his grateful response. He was so positive about his call coming from God, so sure was he of the experience of God's grace, that Francis subjected himself and this grace, whose revelation fell to his lot, to the judgment of the Church. He caused this Gospel life-style, which the Lord had revealed to him for himself and his brothers, *"to be written in few words and simple manner."* With this first Rule he went to Rome to submit it to the Pope for his judgment and approval. *"And the Lord Pope confirmed it to me."* Here gratitude also resounds. It was thanks for the goodness and readiness with which Mother Church took the Lesser Brothers under her care and defended them against all attack, particularly from the bishops of that time. Francis knew what the papal approval of his Rule meant for the movement which it initiated.

However, we do not wish to overlook here how it is almost assumed that the Rule would be mentioned first when looking back to the beginning of the Order. Francis obviously wanted a regulated community right from the beginning, one where a life standard was considered as obligatory on all. Francis strove from the very beginning to give a definite form to the divine call, to the charism he had received. This form must have been very simple.

A Benedictine contemporary of Francis reporting about this first Rule wrote disdainfully, "It can all be written on one page." Next to the Benedictine Rule, the Rule that Francis wrote truly did appear as but one short page. But this Rule reveals itself as the life-giving seed which has lost none of its life-giving power through the centuries. The Gospel form has been and is not only the life and Rule of the Lesser Brothers, but also of the women of the Second Order, the Poor Clares, and of the Brothers and Sisters in the Third Order Regular. It is still today that which determines the form and style of our lives.

After Francis spoke of the Rule which should order our lives, he returned to his historical manner, using a form almost like minutes. It is true that here in this fourth section of the Testament the same thought pattern is found as that in the first chapter of both Rules Francis has given us, and thus one can surely see here in these sentences a reflection of the framework of that original Rule which, unfortunately, was lost. That may be true, but I don't believe it is so important for us. More important is that in the similarity of the aforementioned chapters of both Rules and in the fourth paragraph of the Testament, the significance of the following points is made clear according to the mind of Francis:

— the Rule given him by God and approved by the Pope;
— the renunciation of all earthly goods;
— the common garb for all the Brothers;
— the various Offices, and yet actually one Office, for priests and lay members.

These things date from the very beginning because Francis here looks back to the very first days of his Order — "And after the Lord had given me brethren . . ."

Thus it is clear that Francis, with these brothers who were given to him, wished to follow a religious life in the Church. The theory which is being developed today that Francis wanted only a loose fraternity with no bonds or restrictions cannot stand in the light of these facts. Francis wanted an Order according to the canonical laws of his time — definitely not, we must also emphasize, in the manner of the older orders of monks, but certainly something new. It was not without reason that he appealed to God's revelation, to the sanction of the Church — and yet as an organized religious community

— with a common Rule and life-style;

— with a uniform garb (which, in the Middle Ages, was evidence of an Order's existence);

— with participation in the Church's Prayer of the Hours (Office);

— but without any common property.

Contrary to all modern points of view, and I stress this once again, in order that the historical truth be clear, this means: *in these four elements we have to see even today, with all the great new forms, the most important fundamentals of our Franciscan way of life.*

In this evangelical way of life as he learned it from God's revelation, the first element for Francis was renunciation of all earthly goods. *"And those who came to us to accept this way of life gave to the poor whatever they might have had."* It is interesting here that Francis says, "to accept this way of life." He uses this same expression in the Rule. Whoever comes to the Brothers does not enter a cloister or an abbey, but rather accepts a way of life which is the same for all, a life-style. Whoever comes to the Brothers announces therewith the will to live something together with the Brothers in the Church: *a life according to the Gospel.* Their whole life, then, should reflect the Gospel. Therefore there must be first of all a sign of poverty, namely poverty as

a break with all previous ties of goods and possessions. This break
was not accomplished in just any manner. Goods and possessions
were not just somewhere abandoned, but rather — again in
accord with the Gospel — given to the poor. What the Franciscan
person relinquished should benefit the poor; in the poor he should
give all back to God. Everything that man has belongs to God,
his Creator; of ourselves we have nothing. The renunciation of
goods and possessions is not only a juridical act, but rather a
recognition of the lordship of God. The renunciation in benefit of
the poor is an acknowledgement of the grace-filled reality that we
encounter God precisely in the poor. In both, then, the kingdom
of God is realized.

Now we come to another point, the religious habit, which I believe we want to consider without passion or anger, without agita-
tion from the outset. We know nothing about the appearance of the
uniform garb of the Brothers except that *"they were content with
one habit, quilted inside and out (if they wished),"* i.e., it was
made thicker and warmer because Francis strictly held to one
tunic as is related in the Gospel sending of the Twelve. Rather
than accept a second habit, Francis preferred that the one be made
a little heavier when this was necessary. Furthermore, it was not
drawn together with a leather belt as was customary with the
older monks, but *"with a cord,"* not stylized as they are today
but rather a simple twine as we would call it. Until recently that
was the hallmark of all members of the Franciscan family (and
therefore the American Franciscans were able to name their maga-
zine "The Cord"). All were able to recognize Franciscans by the
cord, but in the meantime this has all been changed.

In addition, each had as a single undergarment, the *"breeches."*
As in the Rule, so here in the Testament, it was more important to
Francis, it seems, to determine the number of pieces of clothing
according to the Gospel. Herein he is quite obviously influenced
by the Gospel account of the Lord's sending of his disciples out to
preach saying they should not put on a second tunic and should
have no shoes nor money in their purses. We know however from
other reports that the clothing of the first friars resembled that of

Francis' own and that it has remained so up until the present.

I believe, if we must hold fast to something, it must be to the viewpoint of poverty. We often discuss the external appearance. It can happen that when someone dies he has a dozen habits hanging in the closet. This is exactly what we want to learn here: it is a matter of poverty — through our clothing we really give witness to the poverty we have promised to the Lord.

That the original tunic soon developed into one obligatory garb the same for all and that it remained so up until the present, we readily admit, and the Church "patented" this garb by canonical prescription. Nevertheless it seems to me we should wear inexpensive clothing; Francis says this even more clearly in the Rule.

In the next sentence the tone is set and to this we wish to pay heed: *"And we had no desire for aught else."* This sentence stands there in utter simplicity — and yet it has crucial meaning. Many, it is true, have given up everything and resemble Francis in dress and in life-style; but then they succumb to the desire-to-have. The desire-to-have and the desire-not-to-have determines and distinguishes: it determines our love to be poor; it distinguishes us from all mankind in the world. Poverty is not just liberation from earthly things; rather — and this will become clear to us here — it is liberation from all desire-to-have; to be those on whom necessity so easily fits. When someone wants to have more, he has his reasons — heaps of reasons. Poverty is not guaranteed by prescriptions, not even in the statutes, but at best by awakening in one a love of the desire-not-to-have. Poverty is an urgent inner attitude of the person, a direction of will, the master of all desire to have this and that and whatever another has.

"For aught else" than that which was necessary to life, *"we had no desire."* This simple sentence, this sign of the attitude of Francis and his first brothers must become for all of us our rule of life: to wish to have nothing more than is necessary to fulfill our tasks and to maintain life. This begins with clothing and ends with the commodities of daily living.

Please do not take me wrong: it is certainly possible for a religious to be more vain in the habit than one in secular dress; it depends on the attitude. Naturally one in secular dress can also be vain, without a doubt. It depends on the internal core. I believe we often discuss too much about the externals instead of being concerned about how the internal core of poverty is being preserved, because precisely today the possibilities of our being tempted are thousandfold. Precisely in the present must we keep this sentence before our eyes: *"And we had no desire for aught else."*

My mother faithfully knitted a pullover for me at least once a year and I never put them on because I didn't need them. Finally, after some years, she stopped doing this and knitted them directly for the poor without making a "detour" through me. One should simply not let such things be pushed upon one. It is a matter of saying, "No, I don't need it," and then giving it to others, becoming thus the means through which those who ordinarily receive nothing can also receive something. We will become acquainted with more of these things when we discuss other points of the Testament. Here it is a matter of fundamental attitude.

The next sentence is: *"The clerics among us prayed the Office like other clerics, while the laics said the Our Father."* From the very beginning Francis inserted himself and his followers into the common liturgical prayer of the Church. Those who could read, that is according to the norms of that time those who understood the written language of Latin, prayed the Divine Office as clerics the same as the other clergy of the Church. The others prayed the prescribed substitute Office composed of Our Fathers as was required by the Rule. This was the prayer that each Christian knew and understood since no prayerbooks existed at that time. It has often been asked whether the first friars prayed the Office together. There is nothing expressly stated about this in the Testament nor in the Rule. We will, of course, come back to this question later in another connection, but it was so from the very beginning. At that time there existed no choir books nor were inexpensive printed breviaries available for purchase. The books necessary for the performance of the Office had to be painstakingly written by hand on expensive parchment. Inexpensive paper as such first appeared much later in the West. Thus the clerics were simply forced by circumstances to pray the Office together, which meant they must go to the churches and join with the clerics there. Francis placed great value on this prayer in common as we will see in parts IX and X of the Testament — and thus it has remained in the Order even to the present day.

"And quite willingly we would live in the churches." This sentence is not just a witness of the piety of the first brothers, but rather it tells us something about their life. From the outset they had no fixed houses except the Portiuncula. Therefore they usually and preferably spent their nights in churches which, at that time, were not locked. In all the transcriptions of the Testament made in the southern lands in the 13th, 14th and 15th centuries this was understood. Only those on the other side of the Alps did not understand; they made it an ascetical matter. "And quite willingly we would live in *abandoned* churches *where no one prayed,"* they wrote. At least one of these transcriptions, from then or later, reads "in *poor and abandoned* churches." But the original meaning was plain and simple: those were their quarters for the night — just as today one often finds men sleeping in doorways. There they prayed and slept when they found no other quarters with some good folk. We can therefore correctly translate the sentence as "And we were willingly content when we had to remain in the churches."

"And we were without learning, and subject to all." In Latin the word "idiotae" is used, but that has nothing to do with the contemporary meaning of the word. Rather, it meant "we had no formal education and so we were simple folk who could only read and write a little," as we know of Francis himself. But to these simple men who were as plain as the first Apostles, a great work was entrusted: *they were called to renew the Church.* And they accomplished this work. Why? "We were subject to everyone, we were ready to serve everyone." They were truly lesser brothers, the kind of menial persons chapter VII of their Rule so gloriously describes. Whether little or seldom heeded, they were to work gladly thus following in the footsteps of their Seraphic Father. This included everything.

Wherever there was need, there they joined in. They helped wherever they found physical or spiritual need. They did not consider themselves too good for any kind of assistance because in their humility they knew they were beneath all others. There was nothing condescending in their service; they did not render assistance from above — "We want to do something for the poor" — but rather as menials they were ready to serve all men, as being beneath them all. This sentence contains in its simplicity a life-time program for each of us: *"We were subject to all."* This is, moreover, based on a saying from the First Letter of St. Peter that applies to all Christians, one which St. Francis often quoted and which was of real concern to him. Thus he shows one of the fundamental principles upon which our Franciscan life-style must be built.

If by way of a practical conclusion we glance back over what Francis said in this fourth part of his Testament, wherein with a few brief but essential lines he drew a picture of how it was in the beginning, then we must admit that the essentials and the decisive points which really matter interiorly and exteriorly have been touched upon.

The interior attitudes are clear:
— gratitude for God's call to a life that is formed by the Gospel;
— gratitude toward the Church who allows us this life-style;
— the will not to have anything beyond necessity;
— preparedness to be of service to all men.

These are the interior attitudes that must animate us.

The formative elements of this life are also clear:
— common Rule;
— renunciation of earthly goods and possessions;
— uniform, and above all poor, clothing;
— prayer in common;
— service of others.

These are the form-giving elements of a Franciscan life-style.

I believe it would be superfluous to say any more. The words of our Seraphic Father are clear, and there remains only one thing for us to do: to think them over again and again so that we con-

tinually begin anew to live them as Gospel-formed persons who —
in genuine minority or lesser-ness — are prepared to serve all.

Almighty and most holy God,
awaken in us that spirit
which inspired your follower St. Francis,
so that we may be filled with that same spirit,
may endeavor to love what he loved, and
strive to bring into reality in our lives
    what he taught.
Through Christ our Lord. Amen.

VII

MANNER OF WORK
(Sections 5 & 6)

The Testament of St. Francis is an exhortation, an encouragement and a reminder which he has left to us as our Founding Father so that we can observe in a more catholic way the Rule which we have promised to the Lord, as he says in one of the later paragraphs. Here, I believe, we must make a fundamental observation: the basic desires of St. Francis are actually very accurately contained also in the Rule of the III Order Regular. Given to the III Order by Pius XI, it is really a compendium, a comprehensive summary, of all the ideas which Francis urged and we will be able to ascertain or, as we have in some instances already, confirm that many points in our consideration of the Testament are also excellent explanations of the III Order Rule. Thus what Francis wrote in his Testament should serve as a guide to our living according to the ideas which he initiated, according to the intentions which are found deposited in the Rule and according to which we have made our profession. And here we must say something which, I grant you, is not "contemporary" for many ears. In the last days of his life Francis was agitated by his great concern that his followers remain firm and true in their regular observance of

135

the life which God had revealed to him. To this he exhorted directly and indirectly. One can actually place the texts of the I Order Rule and of the III Order Rule side by side and find a true spiritual unity. This becomes particularly clear to us as we consider today paragraphs V and VI on work:

"And I was wont to work with my hands, and I still wish to do so. And I earnestly wish that all the friars be occupied with some kind of work, as long as it becomes our calling. Those who do not know how should learn, not indeed out of any desire to receive the pay which the work may bring, but to give a good example and to avoid idleness. And if there are times when no pay is given for our work, then let us have recourse to the table of the Lord, and beg alms from door to door.

"As our greeting, the Lord revealed to me that we were to say: 'The Lord give you peace!' "

We see here how Francis exhorts directly and indirectly as never before in his Testament. He refers first of all to his own example as can be seen in part V. He demands of others nothing that he is not prepared to do himself. We should often refer back to this basic consideration ourselves. As a matter of fact, this is true not only in the Testament but also in his other writings: always his own example comes first and then his request, his exhortation, his demand.

I believe we must look at this 5th paragraph of the Testament along with, coincidentally, the 5th chapter of his I Order Rule and see them in unison. However, if we take the 5th chapter of his Rule, then we must at the same time take the 7th chapter of the Rule of the III Order Regular which repeats almost word for word the 5th chapter of the I Order Rule. Then we will see both promulgations of Francis as one. We must, however, also accept the explanation based on chapter V of the Rule which Francis himself gave in another situation for the students of the Order; this is in the Letter to St. Anthony.

In order to understand all these texts, whether it be the Rule, the Testament, the Letter to St. Anthony or the Rule of the III Order Regular, some pre-considerations are necessary. Just as in ancient times, so also in the Middle Ages "work" meant only manual labor. When we today speak of mental or intellectual work, that is contemporary usage. In the Middle Ages mental labor was never referred to as work and therefore intellectual labor was never respected. One received no pay for this. From mental work one could not directly earn a living. Therefore those who wished to devote themselves to such activity (think only of the professors at the University of Paris) could pursue this way of life only by guaranteeing their existence through ecclesiastical benefits or legal fees (e.g., from real estate) from which they could afford to live as professors since students payed nothing and they received no salaries. An equalization of manual labor and somewhat of studies appeared first in the above-mentioned Letter of St. Francis to St. Anthony in which the Founding Father applied to the study of the friars those principles for manual labor which he had incorporated in chapter V of the Rule — excepting, of course, the prescriptions concerning pay since at that time this simply did not exist for studying.

Since both are again combined in the III Order Rule, because this made a basic change in attitude and practice in the lives and relationships of persons in this regard, today we may without hesitation make use of St. Francis conception of both forms of work — physical and mental-intellectual — not only may, but must. The scope of mental-intellectual labor should not fall outside the scope of that which Francis defined in Rule and Testament.

I would like here to pose a question regarding chapter VII of the III Order Rule: Does the phrase "within the scope of manual labor" play any role at all in the lives of our Sisters? This is a question which we must take very seriously. It says in the I Order Rule: "Those whom the Lord has given the grace of working . . ." We must here keep in mind the total range of activity otherwise for many Sisters an important area of their lives remains untouched by that which Francis intended for his followers — e.g., think only of our teaching Sisters. Therefore we should accept these words of the Testament very seriously.

Francis begins paragraph V of the Testament by saying: *"And*

I was wont to work with my hands and I still wish to do so."
Here Francis first of all gives plain and simple witness that to
him manual labor is an ideal and a value. Since the day of his
conversion he had worked and earned his own livelihood through
manual labor. He still held to this ideal of self-support by manual
work since he felt this was part of the apostolic life and being
a follower of Christ. He held this ideal even to the end of his
life — work being understood, of course, in the broad sense and
not merely working with one's hands.

Francis goes on to say: *"And I earnestly wish that all the
friars be occupied with some kind of work, as long as it becomes
our calling."* Let us notice the relationship of the two sentences.
Francis here demands, as always, nothing from his brothers that
he is not ready to do himself. He first makes the demand of himself and then of the others. This reveals a basic attitude of his life.
He is first concerned that he does something and then follows his
expectation of the others. Let me make this very practical for you:
today we have persons who call for reform. They shout so loud
for reform that they drown out their own consciences. Their demand for reform is an alibi because they are trying to avoid the
reform of their own "I." I believe we can say this in all sincerity
in connection with these words of St. Francis. Whoever is truly
earnest about reform begins with self and not with others. Whoever is really concerned about reform does not begin with the
state of affairs of another, but with the reform of his own heart.
And this is what Francis shows us here quite clearly. We all suffer
today in the Church from those who constantly call for reform and
who at the same time are unwilling to reform themselves; herein
lies, of course, the problem. I believe that Francis shows us here
where a beginning must be made. He began with himself and
thus should we also begin with ourselves.

As we can see, Francis emphatically promotes here the require-
ment of manual labor, in fact for all the friars. He makes only one
restriction: *". . . as long as it becomes our calling."* What is meant
by this and what is ruled out by this cannot be exactly determined
here nor in his other writings. However we surely cannot go

wrong if we assume that such work as does not accord with our Franciscan life of poverty and humility is excluded. This one can clearly and unequivocally demonstrate.

"Those who do not know how," Francis continues, *"should learn."* This prescription must have held a special significance at that time when occupational training was not demanded as much as it is today. Francis wished that his friars should learn a special trade, and I believe he saw here something very accurately because only when one has learned something well does he find that real joy in his work which fulfills a person. This we know from experience: those who are dissatisfied and those who are most easily susceptible to revolutionary ideas are those who do not find fulfillment in their work. We should pay attention to this! We should see to it that every individual finds fulfillment in their work so that they find joy in it. Formerly we had the principle that whenever it was noticed that a Sister was happy in her work she would be transferred and given another job so she could practice humility. God will see to it that humility is practiced; that is not for us to provide and we have received no vocation to that.

". . . not indeed out of any desire to receive the pay which the work may bring," says Francis, *"but to give a good example and avoid idleness."* In this most crucial sentence of the whole paragraph Francis speaks of the motive for working. Here he is concerned with the reason for which Franciscans should work. First of all the desire to receive a good salary is excluded. In regard to this allow me to make some observations here. Today we must relinquish houses — everywhere. It would be very "un-Franciscan" if we gave up houses according to the principle of "What do we get out of it?" *". . . not indeed out of any desire to receive the pay which the work may bring,"* is a very practical instruction. We can see from this that the brothers at the time of Francis worked for others in order to earn their living just as today many religious are employed in works that do not belong to their congregations. Obviously there were among the friars also those who were too much concerned with earnings and profits and so were willing to work only in jobs that paid well. People are people at

any time in history — otherwise Francis would surely not have given this serious admonition.

Following this comes the essential point: *"to give a good example."* I know only too well that today many do not wish to hear of giving a good example. Perhaps we have worn out the expression about giving a good example and thus this opposition to it has arisen. Then let us try to put it into very modern terms. That we should work, not with the desire to receive pay but rather to give a good example, can be said in our plain and contemporary terms as follows: Franciscans should practice among the people the ideal of working without profit. Right at the time of Francis the practice of seeking profit as the main objective of work began. We do not speak without reason of the time of early capitalism in the 12th century. Because of capitalism man was no longer the lord of work but became rather the slave of profit, enslaved by the earnings which resulted. These people who were in danger of losing the Christian purpose of seeking the kingdom of God by their hunger after profit, did a real disservice to the witness of genuine Christian labor. And it was Francis' wish that his friars bring this witness back into Christianity. Naturally it was much easier then than now because they worked more among the people.

Francis gives also a third motive: *". . . and to avoid idleness."* That sounds a little trite, like an eternal platitude. Let us go a little deeper into it. If we look at the prayer of the fourth Canon of the Mass we see it said there that by his work man participates in God's creative act. By working he administers the dominion of God in creation and thus, as God's image and likeness, renders visible the hidden Creator. Work is not a result of original sin — rather, the fact that we find work hard is the result of original sin.

Work as participation in creation is the highest calling of man prior to original sin; and therefore idleness does not present a picture of God but a caricature of God. The vice-ridden person falls into decadence because he is not what he should be. The proverb has good reason to say: "Idleness is the beginning of

vice." It is for this reason that the old catechism listed idleness
with the seven capital sins out of which many others flow. My
father once asked: "Who knows anything today about the seven
capital sins? Who still has a clear grasp, who still knows, where
lie the roots from which all evil grows?" And therefore we can
understand the concern of our Father Francis about this point of
avoiding idleness.

*"And if there are times when no pay is given for our work,
then let us have recourse to the table of the Lord, and beg alms
from door to door."* In these simple words the not-for-profit character of Franciscan work is even more strongly given. The Franciscan person, we'll say it again in our contemporary terminology,
should claim no rights, not even the right of just pay, for the
work performed, as is taken for granted in the working world of
today. If the wages of the brothers should be withheld or are
insufficient to sustain life, then they should beg alms as do other
poor people.

When Francis here uses the deeply meaningful expression of
"the table of the Lord," he opens our eyes to the mystery which
is there hidden. To sit at the table of the Lord, at the Eternal
Banquet, is the predestination of the Christian as the Lord teaches
in the Gospel. For Francis, begging alms is recourse to the Lord's
table, an anticipation of that Banquet, and that is the critical
aspect, that we are allowed to partake without having earned it
on our part. Partaking at this table will be a sign of our predestination, a witness of the world to come. In another place, Francis
says this very clearly: "What in the eyes of the world seems like
foolishness and brings disgrace, will be revealed as the wisdom of
the children of God because these see and judge it from the side
of true wisdom."

We should not overlook the fact, which I believe, is sometimes
overlooked in the history of the Order, that begging appears here
only as an alternative when wages are not sufficient or are not
given at all. Francis positively did not wish that we should live
entirely from begging and should not work, as he once said:

". . . so that we be less of a burden on the people." Idle begging then was not his ideal.

"As our greeting, the Lord revealed to me that we were to say: "The Lord give you peace." (paragraph VI)

Through their work and, of course, on their begging tours, the Friars Minor and, in fact, all Franciscans come into constant contact with other people. They work among them, share in their life, their cares, their joys and sorrows. Just think about a Sister-nurse who has charge of a floor; a Sister-teacher who takes her duty more seriously than just a job to be accomplished; etc. In all these areas we should be servants of peace. That must be our interior concern. Precisely in the work-a-day world where earnings and profits are the main concern, quarrelling, bitter arguments and strife so easily arise. In those houses where Franciscans work discord is so often found. This is just the way it is among men, and it will remain so as long as man is subject to the effects of original sin. Therefore the Lord Himself gave this commission to his disciples as He sent them to announce the Good News of God's kingdom: "When you enter a house, say first: Peace to this house." As disciples sent by Christ, all religious who follow the way of Francis should not only wish peace to all those they meet or with whom they have contact, but, as it says in the Rule, they should bring them peace.

"The Lord give you peace!" should not only be their constant prayer but their incessant endeavor. Whoever is at peace with God, finds peace also with men. In him is fulfilled the words of Christ: "Peace I bequeath to you, my own peace I give you; a peace the world cannot give, this is my gift to you" (Jn 14:27). This is why the world cannot give peace to men.

The dying Francis directed the gaze of his followers toward a very important apostolate — to serve as peace-makers among men. This apostolate is an important requisite for the coming of the kingdom of God, that kingdom of justice, of love and of peace, of which the Church sings in the Preface of the feast of Christ the King. As followers of Francis we are especially called to be servants of this peace. The promotion of peace is one of the most important services which we can perform for Christ the King. Let us again use contemporary terms: the community that works without seeking profit is the community that is without strife. By both these means they bring about the kingdom of God, the kingdom of love and of peace. A community without strife — let that be the subject of our examination of conscience.

We cannot help seeing, therefore, in these two paragraphs, V and VI, of the Testament that Francis gives one important exhortation after another. Even though much that was said was primarily for the Order at his time, I believe we can see therein the time-less core that is valuable and meaningful also for us today. In conclusion let us draw out these points of timeless value and try to put them in more contemporary terms:

1. *Francis did not demand of others what he himself was not willing to do.*

He was deeply convinced that the world would not change if mankind itself did not change and mankind will not change if I myself do not change. Therefore Francis in no way wished to re-form the developments in society, the Church and the general state of affairs, but rather to reform himself. We notice in this section that he wished to lead us to this same attitude. He calls to us, so to speak: "Change yourself! Better yourself! Then change and make better the world!" In this way, without wanting to, without a program, without even thinking about it, he changed the world of his time; perhaps we can do the same today.

And let it once again be clearly said, let us be honest about it: Are not all these searchings for reform of situations and develop-ments often only an alibi because we cannot accomplish a change and reformation in our own lives and we want to deaden our own conscience? Would that we were students of this saint who ac-complished great things because he began radically with himself!

2. *The world of today has no greater need than that of the living witness of Christians who will work selflessly and without profit.*

If someone only asks "What do I get out of it," then self-seeking triumphs further in the world; the kingdom of Satan expands even

more extensively in individual and communitarian life. Work —
and here we include studies, charitable activity, teaching, care of
souls, and also the life of prayer, a life dedicated to the service of
God — work must remain free from this disastrous and embit-
tering question: "What's in it for me?" Never may we in any
instance let our glance turn toward our own profit, but we must
put to ourselves rather the one Christian question: "How can I
serve the kingdom of God in this?" Then all our activity will be
directed toward the service of God, fulfilling a summons from
Him whom we obey without considering whether we are to receive anything from it or not.

   3. *We Franciscans may not consider any kind of work as
      beneath us.*

This is clearly expressed also in chapter VII of the III Order
Rule. The Franciscan should help wherever help is needed,
wherever and however God asks it through obedience — and not
do only that which is regarded as suitable, what is pleasing, what
belongs to a specialized field. The question is rather what the kingdom of God requires, what love and the need of another demands;
this is the here-and-now duty and call of God to the Franciscan.

   Here being without gain or profit also applies — not to seek
honors and recognition from others, to be praised, to find one's
own satisfaction. For us what pertains to work is not that which
is done out of desire or to gain a salary, but rather that which gives
an example — and how much the Christians of today need this
witness we don't have to waste any words explaining. How important chapter VII of the Rule can be for the whole religious
life we also need not waste words explaining; one needs only to
meditate on it, think it through well, and perhaps also discuss it
with one another. Then we can begin to insert such life into the
life of the Church.

   4. *We Franciscans should not divert to ourselves any claims of
      privilege because of our work.*

If it is granted, it should be accepted; if nothing is forthcoming,
this should not make any real difference to us. And here is where
it becomes problematic: to work with the same love, the same

care and concern where no recognition, no thanks, no pay can be expected, just the same as where one is honored by gratitude, by recognition, by salary. Here is where it really begins. Here it is a matter of interior attitude and, I believe, we can see here that this interior attitude of poverty is really the most difficult aspect of Francis' ideal of poverty. He sets it clearly before us: to be content with everything is a fundamental attitude of those who are designated for the table of the Lord. To be satisfied with what God allots us through others — that is realized poverty!

5. *The necessity of our contributing toward peace in the contemporary world and in Christendom is obvious in itself to us.*

Let us remember that we can be servants of peace only when we ourselves build the most strife-free community possible. Here the words of the Rule apply — the peace that is carried in the heart and which should be proclaimed one must first of all have. "The Lord give you peace." This prayerful wish must first of all form, shape and define the relationship of the community members to one another. Through our communities the peace of Christ must convincingly permeate the Church of today.

I need hardly point out that there is much here for all of us to do. We don't need to look for new apostolic activities. Let us fulfill first these which are given us in the Rule and which Francis has clarified in his Testament. I believe here we have very much to do.

Let us close therefore with the wish and prayer for us all that the Lord give us the strength to work without profit and, conflict-free, to contribute to peace, foremost and above all in our own communities and from there into the entire Church and the whole world.

> Most holy and glorious God,
> enlighten the darkness of my heart
> and grant me genuine faith,
> firm hope, and perfect love.
> Give me, O Lord,

true perception and understanding
so that I may fulfill the holy mandate
which in truth has been given me by You.

— St. Francis

VIII

PILGRIMS IN THE WORLD
(Section 7)

The next two parts of the Testament of our Holy Father Francis are very difficult not only for the Friars Minor but even more so for all the other followers of St. Francis because they primarily deal very concretely with the circumstances of that time. However, I believe that precisely from these two sections we can learn something that is valid for all times. The question is how one can gain the full value from them. In order to do this we must first of all clarify the situation of that time, see how Francis behaved and reacted in that situation, and then ask ourselves what meaning it has for us.

First let us take the text of part 7:

"The friars should make sure that they do not receive under any circumstances churches, houses however small and mean, and all else built for their use, unless these are truly in keeping with the holy poverty which we have promised in the Rule; and they should always, as strangers and pilgrims, consider themselves as guests therein."

We know today more than ever that the first brothers of St. Francis were not stationary. True, they had a certain center for their community near the Portiuncula chapel to which they always returned from their apostolic journeys, where they met for their

147

annual chapter and prepared together whatever pertained to the general welfare of the fraternity. During the course of the year, however, they gave witness of the reality that the brothers had no permanent residence. The larger the number of brothers became, the more was the whole impossible to oversee. It frequently happened that individuals went their own way and did not bother anymore about the bond of obedience. The community threatened to break asunder. St. Francis also saw this danger. We know his many and sharp threats against such brothers who dawdled outside the realm of obedience. We also know that he turned to the Pope to procure ecclesiastical decrees of penalty against such brothers. At the same time we also know that all the admonitions and regulations of St. Francis, even though sharply and unrelentlessly worded — we will speak of this again later in the course of the Testament — were not effective. The problem and the danger remained. Also the precautions of the Church did not have the effect at that time that they would perhaps have today. The times themselves were too turbulent for that.

The whole situation was intensified at the end of 1220 when Pope Honorius III, in one of the most difficult crises of the young Order, which was not in the least hampered by the lack of its own mission houses or establishments, introduced the novitiate contrary to the wishes of St. Francis. Now the question of permanent houses for the brothers could no longer be avoided. Francis must take hold of the question and seek to solve it according to the spirit of the Rule. This he does in the seventh part of his Testament.

In order to understand the full weight of this part, we should first of all recall once again this prescription of the Rule:

"The brothers are to take nothing as their own, neither house, nor place, nor any thing."

Here, as in the Rule as such, the fact that the brothers have no residence is adhered to, just as was the case in the attempts of many new orders at that time. We need only think of St. Norbert and the early Praemonstratensians. They were all influenced by these words of the Gospel:

"The Son of Man has no place to lay his head."

They saw this as an essential for the follower of Christ since they were wandering preachers. But all of them came little by little to have permanent establishments.

In its prescriptions, the Testament shows us that even among the Friars Minor a very definite development had also taken place. The brothers accepted churches and residences which however were obviously built for them by others. The most important point actually is this: Francis did not take a position regarding the fact of this development. On the contrary, he recognized this development. His concern now is only that this development be adapted to the spirit of the Rule which should be the basis of the life of his brothers. From this we can rightly conclude that Francis himself was convinced of the necessity of this development. Therefore he did not discuss further whether the brothers should have permanent residences or not. They should have permanent homes but they should take care that they were in accord with the Rule they professed. Thus Francis was decidedly concerned with how the development would proceed. He was not against it, he did not protest it, rather he was concerned that it should be carried out in the spirit of the Rule.

It is precisely this, the manner, which he develops in a two-fold direction:

1. When the brothers accepted establishments with churches and residences which were built for them, Francis wanted to know that a definite limit would be preserved, one that would not be overstepped: that of poverty as it is fundamentally laid down in the Rule and to which the brothers consented at their profession. Here poverty must be preserved so that the brothers do not appropriate anything, nor acquire anything as their own property, nor take anything into their own possession. They may not simply accept that which was built for them.

Immediately the question arises: To whom shall the establishments belong? In his holy indifference, Francis doesn't even ask this question, neither here nor in other places in his writings which deal with similar development. He is sufficiently satisfied that they not belong to the brothers. Perhaps he simply wishes to leave the right of ownership to the donor so that the brothers live only as tenants as he himself was accustomed and also, for example, the brothers in England. He did not concern himself with it so that danger to the Church's own rights was again brought on, an abuse from which the Church in the Middle Ages had just freed itself through a monstrous struggle — namely, when a nobleman or a sovereign built a church, it belonged to him. He appointed the priests and collected the revenues. The hierarchy had absolutely no influence over these churches. Right at this time the abuse of these private churches had been eradicated, an abuse which had brought the Church into a disgraceful dependence on worldly might and power — somewhat like when the Emperor appointed one of his functionaries as abbot in the imperial abbey; this one collected the revenues and let the abbey run itself.

Precisely this point was the concern of Cardinal Ugolino, later Pope Gregory IX. He saw very clearly the danger which in the future brought disaster on the brothers in many places. For example, in England they hit upon the following solution: we will give all to the civil authorities and the city will then be the owner. When, in the 16th century the Reformation came, the civil authorities claimed all their own properties and the brothers were left out on the streets or could leave the country. This danger existed but Francis certainly did not recognize it. Therefore in 1230 Gregory IX decreed that at least all churches built for the Friars Minor were to be made the property of the Holy See and the residences only when the donor did not retain the right of ownership himself. Thus it was prevented that the Order should fall into dependence upon secular powers which could make it impossible for them, as in the aforementioned case, to fulfill their ecclesiastical duties.

Many of the so-called cloister council rooms of the Order in Medieval times were the halls of celebration for the City Council. There they held their council meetings and there the council celebrations where held. That this was very bad for the religious, we are also aware. Thus there was only one possibility remaining at that time — that the brothers accept, of course, the missions but the right of ownership was taken over by the Church. So we can see in this case, as in so many others, that Francis suggested and corrected developments whose valid incorporation into the life of the Church he left to the competent authorities. To him it was sufficient that the brothers were not property owners. How it would be in the future he left to its own development.

2. Francis laid a decisive value on the brothers' maintaining their missions in the proper spirit. In their apostolic wandering they presented clearly and visibly that early Christian truth that the Christian is a pilgrim and a stranger to this world and its times. They should have no permanent resting places. They should not establish themselves domestically so that by their homeless presence they witness to the next life.

Thus Francis presented it clearly in the sixth chapter of the Rule and quoted I Peter 2 that the brothers should serve the Lord in poverty and humility "as pilgrims and strangers in this world." Here in his Testament he quotes again these words of the Apostle. In their establishments the brothers should also recognize themselves as only pilgrims and strangers. He underscored this attitude further in the sentence: they should consider themselves as guests.

A guest has no right of ownership, no right of disposition over the room in which he dwells nor over the furnishings found in it. He is happy that he has a place to stay for a little while, but does not reckon with remaining. He is happy with what he finds there and with what the goodness of others provides for him. All this the brothers should observe even when they live in permanent establishments. They should be educated and trained in all of this.

We might well say that when Francis, in this section of the Testament, juridically, sufficiently, unconcernedly solved the problem of a stationary existence, settled it for a future even less capable of bearing the burden, he masterfully solved this new situation according to the spirit of the Rule and according to the original spirit of the New Testament. With a few strokes he sketched the fundamental attitudes which would remain forever valid for the Franciscan family.

Recall that in the Rule of the Third Order Regular the idea of Christians in pilgrimage is also used. We should present that aspect of the Church as pilgrim Church by our total attitude toward life. This fundamental attitude is directed precisely toward the goal of St. Francis who writes his Testament as a reminder, an admonition, an exhortation so that we will more thoroughly observe the Rule by which we have promised the Lord to live.

If today in the present circumstances, in our own situation, we would like to observe the Rule in the spirit of Francis, we will always have to pay attention to the explanation of the poverty question which he himself gives here in his Testament. We will also need to be continually careful that in our housees, primarily in each private cell or room, that all that we have "is in accord with the holy poverty which we have promised in the Rule." The greatest obligation of the child is to imitate the virtues of his father and therefore the Third Order religious should especially strive to live well the final paragraph of the Rule which speaks of the poverty and love of the Seraphic Father.

I believe that we must all be more alert here that we do not take as our gauge that which is permissible for those outside religious life, outside the Order, the contemporary standard in society. We are always confronted with an examination of conscience. Precisely here we must be careful that our private living quarters do not match that style of middle-class Christianity which serves only ease and comfort. If so, then we have in reality rejected the essence of our poverty. We must continually check everything according to the measure of a Franciscan life — and the most important point therein is this fundamental sentence of the Testament: all must be "in keeping with the holy poverty which we have promised in the Rule."

It is not without purpose that Francis here appeals to our intention which we once made known publicly at our profession as we obligated ourselves before God and the Church to live the Rule of one of the Franciscan Orders for our entire lifetime. This solemn promise must be lived out in our daily lives. This promise must be realized, insofar as it is related to poverty, in our living quarters and our cells, particularly in their furnishings. Francis knew, as is obvious in his Testament, of the grave danger of our forgetting and taking on the life style of the world. The "life style of the world" must be understood in this context in its comprehensive and broad sense.

As Franciscans we have left the world; therefore we do not need to have everything that persons outside the cloister can have, whether it be a matter of food and drink, dress or other commodities, or a question of going to theatres and movies, use of the radio and television, attendance at lectures and whatever performances are offered. Must we also have all of this? Understand me correctly now: when it is something that serves our apostolic activity — yes! But when it is simply a matter of also having or doing because others have or do it, then we must ask the question: Is this necessary? Then we must honestly ask: Do I need this? Should we not all reflect anew here on the challenge of the Apostle: "Do not put on the things of this world." Literally translated this means do not adopt the form, the life style, of this world.

By living according to our Rule, as Francis urges in this exhortation of his Testament in imitation of the Apostle Paul, Franciscans should be a living witness that Christ is not of this world. And I believe here we must continually reflect together on what we really need. The Council (Vatican II) obligated us to make precisely this consideration. And what we do not need, that we should not use.

Thomas of Celano once pertinently said of Francis: "This man hates not only the arrogant vanity of houses, but he especially has an intense abhorrence for numerous and choice household utensils." All this should proclaim our pilgrim life, our exile.

It is furthermore not a matter of being purely economical, but rather we are aware

— that we are Christians in pilgrimage;
— that as Christians we must continually keep ourselves available;
— that we do not become permanent residents.

How many are in a sense "married" to their houses and cells so that they cannot even move from one floor to the other — even when it is necessary. I dare say, here is sin against the three vows: against obedience because they will not let themselves be moved; against poverty because one believes that one has right of ownership for this job or this house or this cell; and against chastity because one feels "married" to it. Celibates sometimes hang their hearts on such things and cling to them with all their might. Therefore I believe Francis was right when he said everything should proclaim our pilgrimage, our exile; we should always be as guests, as pilgrims and strangers.

There are enough instructions and admonitions given, and sufficient grounds pointed out to preserve us Franciscans from uniformity with this world and to strengthen us in our love of being poor as is asked by our Rule.

When the development into cloistered living in its true sense became necessary for the young Order — and it has remained necessary for it even up to today — Francis gave a genuine regulation for this development by which he showed us how we can remain true to our own ideal even within the need for permanent establishments.

This will become more apparent and clear to us when we interpret more practically the second regulation for this development that Francis here describes with the words:

"They should always, as strangers and pilgrims, consider themselves as guests therein."

We are then in the convent, in our cell, guests who live in property belonging to another. This naturally has the effect that we handle with care everything in the convent and in our rooms as something belonging to another, not acting as owners but as someone to whom something has been entrusted for use, even to the extent that we treat things as one delicately handles what belongs to a stranger. It does not belong to me.

The fact that in our convent and in our rooms we are but guests has by nature the further effect that we do not cling to our room nor to its furnishings. We should be prepared at any time to separate ourselves from it if it is necessary. Every superior today freely makes broad consideration of our respective wishes. I hardly believe that our superiors would rudely interfere in these matters; I almost said, would dare to interfere. — What a poverty-witness of our interior spiritual attitude that one can no longer dare touch it! For this reason I believe that we must educate our own consciences the more so. Precisely in regard to these questions must we arrive at a genuinely Franciscan conscience. And that is the question that presents itself to us now. Let us recall the last chapter of the Rule of the Third Order Regular which speaks of persons in pilgrimage, of love for poverty.

— Is our conscience sufficiently sensitive regarding these questions? — or the reverse?
— Do we make a matter of conscience the things we use and the things we have in our room?
— Are we convinced that we should only be guests, only pilgrims and strangers?

I used to say to my novices, "Once a year do a thorough house-cleaning in your cell; pick up every thing and look at it. If you have not used something for a whole year, then you do not need it. Then we will put all these things together." We usually did this during Christmastime or during Advent and were able to send many packages to the East Zone. It was a very healthy practice! I don't know how it is with women, but bachelors hang on to everything saying: You never know when you might need it for something. And then they collect all sorts of things. If I have not used something for a whole year, then I give it away!

I believe we must form our consciences in this, because no conscience will form itself. If we do not practice something concretely, train it, then we cannot wonder why we have no criteria or positive measuring stick.

A third point here must also be observed. We know that as Christians, we in particular as Franciscans, should be living witnesses that we have no permanent dwelling but, as one prefers to say today, that we are disposable — unattached and available. We speak much today about disposability or availability as a modern form of poverty — but oh my! when someone wishes our availability! Then the whole discussion is closed. Here too it is a matter of interior attitude.

How many have not been able to overcome themselves for years, or even for a lifetime, so that they could be transferred from a place where, as I have said, they cling with all their hearts. This is not living "as pilgrims and strangers." Particularly today, the Church has a need of exactly this witness — that there are persons who do not cling to things, persons who are free as pilgrims and strangers — above all in our countries with their high standard of living. I believe herewith something very decisive is being said regarding our Franciscan life in community.

Perhaps we can sum it up in this way: developments in the Church and in the Order are inevitable. There is nothing human that remains at a given point. Or one must live like the Carthusians, completely enclosed. But not everyone can do this and this is not our vocation. Therefore we are always in the midst of development. That we can see already during the lifetime of St. Francis. The need for studies and formation for the brothers was then already evident. The need for definite residences and their own churches was obvious. Francis did not set himself in opposition to necessary developments but — and this is the important point — he understood the new developments in the light of the fundamental principle of a life according to the Rule, a life according to the Gospel which would be incorporated, formed from within the community and not that each went his own way, but at the same time allowing the good will of individuals sufficient freedom of expression. The same is true here.

One wishes that the direction here recognized would be observed more and more by the Franciscan family. Then precisely
— through our simplicity,
— through our being pilgrims,
— through our poverty
we would remain a living witness of the life to come for the Church and world of today, of that life toward which we are all moving.

IX

TOTAL POVERTY
(Section 8)

The next section of the Testament of our holy Father Francis reads:

"I firmly command all the friars by obedience that, wherever they may be, they do not dare to ask for any letter of privilege at the Roman Curia, either directly or through intermediaries, whether concerning a church or any other place, or under the pretext of preaching, or even as protection against persecution. Rather, if they have not been welcomed in one place, let them depart to another and there do penance with the blessing of God."

No point in the entire writings of St. Francis created such a stir in the history of his Order as this section of his Testament. This prohibition distinguished the true sons of Francis from the so-called Spirituals of the Middle Ages. It created diverse reactions and divisions. Unfortunately many hot-heads, especially within the radical circle of the Spirituals, saw in this a license on the basis of which they rejected all obedience to the Church. This was definitely tragic. Often in their onesided striving to be true sons of St. Francis, they became caught up in the letter of the law and lost the essential element of a Franciscan life: obedience and subjection to the Roman Church and her Head, the Pope.

Many modern Franciscan scholars, particularly among the Protestants, have based their opinions and remarks on this section of the Testament, overrating it and utilizing it onesidedly for their own intention. Thus it was, perhaps, that the Protestant pastor Paul Sartre saw here evidence that Francis saw through the politics of the Roman Curia and rejected them in flaming protest. Another sees in this instance a most severe accusation against the curial system of governing which rested precisely upon privilege in its broadest sense. This opinion has not died out even today. We need only think about the latest Franciscan book by Mario von Galli which is thoroughly saturated with the spirit of Paul Sartre — although von Galli himself admits in his foreword that he was unable to make the great effort of studying first the written sources. His book does not present Francis.

In contrast, the Order has maintained that all the emerging difficulties be solved by the Apostolic See and that all controversies that arise be settled by them. This was accomplished naturally and according to the custom of the Curias through letters of commendation or privilege. Who was right in regard to this question — the Spirituals and their followers or the Order in its entirety down to the present? This is truly a problem. Even though it is not so urgent a problem for us today, it is still a problem. We have here an important expression of the will of our Founding Father before us, one which, if we may say so, we cannot simply by-pass in all innocence. But in this case, by way of example also perhaps for other similar questions, let us calmly gather together all the facts:

— It is certain that in many of the difficulties of the young Order Francis turned to Rome and let them be settled by papal briefs.

— It is just as certain that he accepted privileges, even important privileges, because they were seen as necessary for the internal life of the Order and its work in the Church.

— It is also certain that he allowed the way of life of the Friars Minor, as it is defined in the Rule, to be approved and safeguarded through papal letters of commendation or privilege.

Francis, therefore, had actually made use of this instrument. What then is the meaning of this strongly worded prohibition?

We know that at that time there were brothers in the Order who wanted from the Pope a general permission to preach so that they could announce the Word of God everywhere independently of the priests and bishops. They did not want to ask anyone, but rather wanted to follow their own discretion. That goal seems to be good and ideal; it really appears to be demanded for the salvation of souls; but Francis would not allow it. He strongly forbids the acquiring of "letters of privilege under the pretext of preaching." He saw herein the danger for the "minority" or "lesserness" of his followers. A Lesser Brother should serve and help others by his apostolic activity. The Lesser Brothers should never appear as lords who should handle and settle things on their own initiative.

Oftentimes, as we know from the chronicles, the Lesser Brothers were persecuted, mistreated and even imprisoned, being taken for heretics — and that is never a pleasant thing! The solution seemed to be to appeal to the Pope for letters of privilege — for the Pope was the most powerful person in Western Christendom. Thus these followers of Francis forgot the words of his Rule that they should preserve humility and patience in persecution and illness and should love those who persecute, rebuke and accuse them. They forgot something very important in their Gospel life. They forgot that about which the Lord spoke so clearly in his Sermon on the Mount and to which Francis often referred: "Love your enemies and pray for those who persecute and calumniate you." "Blessed are those who suffer persecution for the sake of justice, for theirs is the kingdom of heaven."

Therefore the dying Francis, for the sake of the Gospel life, here strictly forbade the acquisition of papal briefs "even as protection against persecution."

It also happened at that time that the Friars Minor sometimes were not received by civil authorities, not even by some bishops, and sometimes were even banished by them. That often must have been hard since they had to construct their poor houses and small churches themselves at great effort. The Pope had not yet taken these over as property of the Holy See. How easily the worldly nobility and the Church authorities could interfere and expel the propertyless Brothers. It is humanly understandable that the brothers sought to protect themselves against such arbitrary action by turning to the higher authority of the Roman Curia. On the other hand, Francis saw here the danger to true lesserness, to the mystery of total poverty which he loved so much. Therefore, in his concern for the internal life of the Order, he forbade the acceptance of such letters of privilege whether for a church or for any one of the houses. *"Rather, if they have not been welcomed in one place,"* the brothers should *"depart to another and do penance there with the blessing of God."*

I believe that the entire sense of this point with its deepest meaning is here revealed to us beyond all the qualifying circumstancs of the times which we have here briefly given.

— A life of penance — this will mean that a person no longer asks for himself.

— A life of penance — this will mean that a person does not ask according to his personal wishes or desires, but rather in a genuine conversion of heart seeks the will of God.

However, God does not reveal his will directly but rather through intermediate causes, through human circumstances which serve to bring about his great purposes. Francis once wrote to a superior, a brother who became tired of his office because everything was too burdensome, because all fell upon him as is so often the case, and therefore he had turned to Francis and said he would prefer to go to a hermitage where he could serve God better than in this office. Francis wrote to him: "This is my advice with regard to the state of your soul." And now comes the advice which really characterizes the life of penance: "As I see it, you should consider everything that makes it difficult for you to love God as a special favor, even if other persons, whether friars or not, are responsible for it, or even if they go so far as to do you physical violence. This is the way you should want it to be. . . . I am convinced that this is true obedience. . . . This should be of greater benefit to you than the solitude of a hermitage."

This is the radical turning away from self: this exposing of oneself to the will of God, however and wherever it manifests itself through whatever circumstances, or even God's permissive willing of what is absolutely displeasing to us or our way of thinking. To look to God's guidance and disposition in all of life's situations whatever they may be, to allow God's plans and arrangements freedom in all life's circumstances, that is an essential element of the Franciscan Gospel life of penance.

Thus Francis wishes that his followers should not try to protect themselves against such guidance and disposition on God's part, against his plans and arrangements, not even by means of papal letters of privilege. This is the deepest meaning of this expression in Francis' Testament.

The Franciscan should nowhere establish himself permanently — in no task, in no activity, in no location — but rather always keep himself freely available to God. The Franciscans should always be prepared to lead a life of penance anywhere and everywhere.

To live a life of penance is not limited to any place, nor restricted to any activity, but rather it can be grasped and realized anywhere. Here we see precisely how deeply the sense of parts VII and VIII are intertwined even though at first glance they appear to have nothing to do with each other. As we saw in the previous section, the followers of St. Francis should live in their houses as strangers and pilgrims, not as lords and owners against whom no one can have any claim. As we tried to explain this section in terms of today's circumstances, we saw that *their life should always have a certain insecurity.* Along with this insecurity, the characteristic feature of Franciscan poverty, uncertainty appears in section VIII of the Testament, *an uncertainty without which poverty would not be genuine.* But this uncertainty, just as the insecurity, makes us free and available for God's will as followers of Christ in its greatest sense.

In both these sections of the Testament, Francis expresses this freely in the language of his times. He says it in terms of the situation in his community at that time. We must try to translate it into our times and our circumstances. It should mean that through this insecurity we are always available as instruments in God's Hand so that regardless of the circumstances, He can place us and use us wherever He wills and whenever it seems good to Him.

At this point we should not forget how this section became a reality for us about 100 years ago. It was impossible at that time to lead a Franciscan religious life in our homeland (Germany). Our Brothers and Sisters did not ask Rome for letters of privilege then — they would have been useless anyway — but rather they departed for other lands there to do penance, to live the penitential life in other circumstances and other situations. They did this in such a way that the life of the Church had a new beginning not only in Germany but also in other places. (Sometimes I like to say that, contrary to his own designs, Bismarck was the founder of many provinces in many countries. Perhaps because of this he made it into heaven!). The Lord proceeds according to his own will even when we cannot comprehend it.

So what at first glance appeared to be a sterile statute with all its minute details as they appear in section VIII, comes forth at closer scrutiny as a very important, pertinent and constantly fruitful reference for Franciscan living. We can say with full authority that this rejection of papal briefs is deeply grounded in the very purpose of the Franciscan life. We can also say with full right — I believe we are now in agreement on this — that it has nothing, absolutely nothing, to do with rebellion against the Church and her system. *This reference is a simple and natural consequence of Franciscan love for total poverty; for that poverty which goes further than being poor in earthly goods; for that poverty which will have no right, no security, no special status, not even in the Church, but which rather leaves utilization and disposition completely to God.*

The example of Bismarck shows us that papal letters of privilege are of no avail today. They would not protect us against the wantonness of worldly power; they would not even help us much among Christians. Hardly anyone would pay any attention to them. Therefore there is hardly a follower of Francis who would today even think about asking one from the Roman Curia. Is this section therefore one of only historical interest to us? Can we therefore, given our completely different circumstances of today, pass over it to today's concerns? It seems to me, and some of our references have already pointed it out, that we should not answer too lightly or too quickly such and similar questions. In this instance it is true that the letter of the law is redundant as it is given, but whoever is not caught up in the literal reading of it will find here a timelessly valid reference for a genuine, true, Gospel-oriented life of penance.

Let us then in conclusion draw out and consider the timeless values found in this section:

1. Behind many phrases of this section is the implicit will of Francis for peaceableness. Our holy Father Francis knew exactly how the defense of ownership, often even just the assertion of ownership and position, leads to quarrels and strife. He wishes to promote peace. He lived this prescription exactly according to what the Lord preached in the Sermon on the Mount: "Give to everyone who asks you, and do not ask for your property back from the man who robs you" (Lk 6:31).

Francis took Jesus' demands seriously: "To the man who takes your cloak from you, do not refuse your tunic" (Lk 6:29). "If anyone orders you to go one mile, go two miles with him" (Mt 5:41). What does this mean? Whoever wants to promote peace dare never rely on rights but must rather be prepared to renounce everything and to offer everything for the sake of love. Perhaps here we have the deepest sense of that part of Chapter V of the Third Order Rule where it is said that the Brothers and Sisters of the Third Order should always promote peace. — Yes, whoever wants to work for peace must be prepared to walk the lower road for the sake of love and peace. That is what is expressed here in the language of the 13th century. One must be prepared to be used. It reminds us of Francis' words to the guardian of the brothers. He must be prepared to suffer injustice patiently.

We all know that this is not easy — the cost of conquering self, of renunciation and offering is high. And, let us dare say it today even though many do not wish to hear it, it costs self-denial. In the past one called this asceticism — without which a Christian life is absolutely impossible. This demands renunciation of self, saying no to oneself — but only in this way is that life whose form is the Gospel of Christ accomplished.

Here we must naturally ask: how are our contemporary circumstances similar to those present to Francis in his day? Of course, this is different in every location; each community must discover this for itself. Yet we cannot evade this question. We must accept an uncertainty here also for the sake of peace.

2. *Francis demands peaceableness from us above all when it concerns our apostolic work. It is precisely in the apostolate, whether it be charitable, pedagogical or pastoral, that we should not claim rights nor rely on privileges.*

As historian of the Order, I can here only say that had the Friars Minor observed this admonition through the course of our history, many arguments and enmities, many rivalries which caused untold damage to the kingdom of God in homeland and missions would have been avoided. That we must admit. As genuine lesser ones we should be ready to serve all — especially in our apostolic activity.

Thus will this section of the Testament serve as a constantly valid admonition for peaceable subordination to all in the Church for, as Francis once said, we are all in the same house which is the Church. Therefore a greater renunciation is demanded of us. But Francis is deeply convinced, as he once said without a doubt to his brothers, that from this renunciation of person grows a greater healing than when we wrestle with another over rights.

3. I have often said, and I repeat again, Francis knew the person, Francis knew also the friar; and that I would now like to take up, but not limit it to men. It is not without reason that we read here in this section, *"under the pretext."* Francis knew that *in our human weakness we would again and again try to secure ourselves against God's guidance and permissive will with plausi-*

ble and even very pious-sounding reasons — just as that guardian who wanted to serve God in a hermitage just to get away from the difficulties of his office.

It is precisely religious-minded persons who easily fall into the danger of relying on pious pretexts in order to gain their own will counter to God's will. Entrenched behind the wall of pretext, behind their mask of piety, they are iron-clad and no longer open and free to allow God to have complete authority over them as He wills. This position is very dangerous when they seek to safeguard themselves by ecclesiastical measures against unpleasantness and vexations. Then the general interest of the Church, the general interest of the community or even of a local house must suffer so that one's individual interest is achieved through such disguised means. — Let us not use such pretexts in order to avoid things which are or can be unpleasant for us. Precisely then let us remain strong and courageous in our following of Francis in a life of penance, distancing ourselves from our own selves.

4. The next point is perhaps very difficult for us. *Francis demands here,* and he does it repeatedly, *that man, the Christian, expose the visible and the invisible enemy.* He is convinced in faith that our enemy can do nothing to us, as he himself says, over and above what God permits. Here he expresses an unbounded faith. And we?

— If we find contrary circumstances or an adverse situation somewhere which does not suit us, do we seek to be transferred?

— If we run up against misunderstanding and rejection, do we run away?

— If we are unable to push through what we believe at the moment to be right, are we quarrelsome and angry, do we withdraw in resentment?

To tolerate a situation, to endure it in faith, to overcome it in a Christian manner, to hold up under it, in every situation to maintain oneself as a Christian, as a person of penance — *this is what Francis demands of us* in this statement. Only when a person has this interior attitude is God able to work through them in all situations and circumstances. It is only then that we will have the one wish and desire as Francis himself expressed it:

— to be what God wills us to be,
— to do what God wills us to do,

and that alone is wholeness or perfection.

In this entire section it is quite evident to us that the words of our Father Francis are not always the most popular with us. That we readily admit. However, it is also clear that when we think them over repeatedly and earnestly try to heed them, to live them in our circumstances and in our times, then they give us spirit and life.

And when we open ourselves without reservation and resentment to these words of our Father Francis, accepting them readily and willingly, they will assist us to truly live our vocation so that our community will become more and more fruitful in the Church as a fraternity of penance because these words lead us deep within the life of penance so that from day to day we become more genuine Franciscans.

Let us pray with our holy Father Francis:

Most holy and glorious God,
enlighten the darkness of my heart
and grant me genuine faith,
firm hope and perfect love.
Give me, O Lord,
true perception and understanding
so that I may fulfill the holy mandate
which in truth has been given me by you.

X

PERFECT OBEDIENCE
(Sections 9 & 10)

The two sections, 9 and 10, of the Testament of our holy Father Francis comprise an inner unity. They treat of two topics which, for Francis, are always closely related to one another, that is to say, he speaks in one breath of praying the Office, the Prayer of the Hours of the Church, and of obedience toward superiors, toward the way of life we have promised to God. These are things we are not likely to join of ourselves. We will also see, as a reflection of Francis' own concern, that his brothers remained orthodox. Praying the Office was then, as it is today, a concrete expression of obedience to the Church.

At that time the heretical Cathari, who rejected the Old Testament from which the greater part of the Office is taken, simply cast the Office aside. Obediently praying the Hours according to the prescriptions of the Rule, that is, according to the regulations of the Church of Rome, was for Francis an expression of union with this Church, a concrete expression of "being Catholic" as Francis so clearly states at the begining of part X.

Both topics will be treated in the same manner as part V of the

Testament and, just to mention in passing, as in the testament of St. Francis for the Poor Clares.

Francis always made demands of himself first. He obliged himself to do whatever he wished to demand of another; then he first turned toward the brothers or sisters. In contrast with part V about manual labor, which we have already considered together, Francis here adds to the demands on the brothers an inflexibly strict sanction through which we meet an heretofore unknown aspect of Francis.

Today we shall concern ourselves only with the aspect of obedience which takes up most of part IX and which is applied to the brothers in the beginning of part X. Let us turn to the text:

9. "And it is my firm desire to obey the Minister General of this brotherhood, as likewise the guardian whom it has pleased him to give me. And I wish to be a prisoner in his hands, so that I can neither move nor act apart from obedience to him and without his consent, because he is my master. And though I am simple and ailing, I wish always to have a cleric who may recite the Office with me, as it is prescribed in the Rule."

10. "And all the friars are to be bound in like manner to obey their guardians . . ."

Precisely these two sections of the Testament, IX and X, written as if to forestall it, are witnesses of that tragedy under which Francis suffered during the last years of his life. It was not a conflict with the Church as has been spoken of from the time of Paul Sabatier, the French Franciscan scholar, down to the latest book by Fr. von Galli, S.J. It was rather the conflict between the ideal of St. Francis and the real life performance of so many brothers. While the oftspoken drama between Francis and the Church did not occur in reality, he did actually suffer from his deep concern about the life of so many brothers who could not follow him in his transcendent call; perhaps, too, many did not want to follow. Moreover — and this we must readily admit — Francis is not entirely without blame in this development.

The responsibility for the continually growing number of brothers was too great for Francis. One must realize that in eleven years the number of brothers increased from 12 to over 3,000, or possibly, if one can believe it, over 5,000. Where could one find formation personnel? From where did one draw the leadership? This increasing number was a problem in the face of which Francis, as he himself admits, did not feel qualified to handle. The responsibility was too much for him and therefore he appointed a delegate who would take care of organizational matters in his name. Unfortunately he called his substitute, here and in the next section of his Testament, Minister General, that is, with the title of office of the highest superior of the Order under whom he also wished to place himself; to whom, however, he also imparted commands in strict obedience, as we shall see.

So it came about that, added to the problem of the rapidly increasing number of brothers for whom it was almost impossible to provide a basic formation, there arose the problem of uncertainty regarding rights because Francis, in his striving for virtue, should, or must, at one and the same time, be the subject and the superior. The question facing the brothers was: who is the competent superior? Here we should have a sympathetic understanding for the task of Brother Elias which was truly not easy, one which he masterfully discharged in that he really understood Francis and accepted the task at his bidding; furthermore, he marvelously resolved the problem of organization in the expanding brotherhood. That abuses also arose from this is fully understandable; and that Francis, in the face of these abuses, did not remain inactive, is also understandable. When he places such stress on obedience, it is a sign that he kept in touch with the development of the whole after as well as before.

Nevertheless, one must say that part IX of the Testament does not contain the whole of Francis' teaching on obedience. Perhaps he was reacting strongly here to the worst abuses of which he heard during the last days of his life. As we are well aware, Francis had a typically impulsive Italian temperament; there, in order to be just, it is necessary to draw together and to see together all his expressions regarding obedience. Otherwise one cannot do him justice. But then, it can also be established that the attitude of

Francis toward obedience had its own growth and development —
a development which was continually oriented toward practical
experience.

In both Rules which he gave the brothers, the precept of obedience is always limited for the subordinate through some addition
as in the following:

> "And all my other blest brothers shall be careful to obey them
> in matters that concern the welfare of their soul and are not
> contrary to our way of life." (I Rule 4)

or "Wherefore, I command them strictly to obey their ministers
> in everything which they have promised the Lord to observe
> and which is not against their soul and our Rule." (2 Rule 10)

On the other hand, to the ministers it is said:

> "The brothers who are ministers and servants of the other
> brothers, shall . . . not enjoin(ing) on them anything that
> may injure their soul or our Rule." (2 Rule 10)

Herewith Francis would proclaim a point of great importance:
both rendering obedience and requiring obedience must be em-
bedded in the gospel way of life as is described by the Rule which
we, by our profession, have decisively accepted as our life. He is
here further stating that rendering obedience and requiring obedience must promote the unconstrained work of God in the life of
the individual and therefore dare not place a hindrance between
God and the soul of the individual. As ideal as this view is, there
still remains the weighty question of who decides what is contrary
to our life, contrary to our Rule and above all, injurious to the
soul. When one considers that sinful man, the sin-burdened person,
lives continually out of his own personhood with all his own
weaknesses concentrated within, then one is tempted to ask
whether the door is not left open to subjective caprice, especially
when one realizes that no Rule and no constitution can concretely
regulate every possible practical situation.

Francis did not see this problem clearly because only two years
after writing the Rule of 1221, he shortened the Rule to half its
original size. In view of this fact, the problem became even more
acute.

In comparing Francis' statement in his Testament regarding this question with his expression in the Rule, one can see immediately that Francis here promises and demands an obedience which, we can readily admit, is similar to the obedience of a cadaver as he himself once illustrated it using the image of a corpse:

"And I wish to be a prisoner in his hands, so that I can neither move nor act apart from obedience to him and without his consent, because he is my master."

We can immediately add to this the first sentence of part X:

"And all the other friars are to be bound in like manner to obey their guardians . . ."

Here we no longer have discussion of some kind of restrictions in the Rule. It is perfectly clear that Francis speaks of a much more rigorous interpretation of obedience here than he did in the Rule. Here we cannot help but ask how many sad and bitter experiences must this man have had in his lifetime — he to whom man's direct relationship with God was perfectly obvious — that such a development was possible, even to the point of necessity, for him.

Yet we are not groping completely in the dark here, He himself speaks of this experience in an important letter which he addressed to all the brothers of the Order, the "Letter to the General Chapter and to All the Friars." In it Francis pointedly distances himself from such brothers — and I quote exactly — "who go roving about, to the disregard of the regular discipline of the Rule." He vigorously exclaims, "I do not want to see or speak with them until they repent." The brothers referred to here had openly misused the interpretation of obedience as Francis had presented it in the Rule. Therefore in the same letter he refers in all earnestness to the committed obedience of Christ:

"Our Lord Jesus Christ gave his life rather than fail in the obedience he owed his most holy Father."

If the brothers wish to observe the holy Gospel of our Lord Jesus Christ, which should be their life style according to their profession, then they must follow in his footsteps, above all in obedience. One feels here, as it were, how Francis tried earnestly to exhort to sanctification such brothers as erred by interpreting the Rule too literally.

This becomes even more obvious if we consider at the same time the third admonition of our holy Father Francis. The mind of Francis is obvious from the text here and again in chapter 5 of the earlier Rule.

Under pretext of being better able to know what was "against their soul and the Rule," many brothers made use of the freedom granted in the Rule and withdrew themselves from obedience in such a way that they separated themselves from superiors and also from the other brothers and led a life according to their own discretion; or, as Francis says in another place, "those who deviate from the precepts of the Lord and wander throughout the world outside the realm of obedience." This was much easier in the Order at that time than it was in later years or perhaps even today, because the brothers did not yet have permanent houses but rather went about the world in groups as wandering preachers or day laborers. One could easily separate himself from the community of brothers and really go his own way. Francis tried to deal with this difficulty in his third admonition:

"And if ever a subject finds anything better and more useful for his soul than what his superior orders, let him nevertheless sacrifice his will to God and set himself to suit his actions to his superior's wishes."

Francis here holds strictly to what he said in the Rule:

"Should a superior, however, give a subject an order that is contrary to his conscience, then though he do not obey him, the subject should not abandon him; . . ." (Admonition 3).

And here again follows a reference to the obedience of Christ:

"For a person that would sooner suffer persecution than be parted from his brethren, certainly abides in perfect obedience, since he is staking his life [as Christ did] for his brethren" (Admonition 3).

Here we also see how Francis, from the aspect of being a follower of Christ, or to put it more concretely, because of his call to a life according to the Gospel, wanted to prevent any hazard in the life of the brothers.

Meantime, he also had to learn from experience — from experiences which, at the beginning of his life with the brothers, had surely never occurred to him as possible. That these experiences were bitter and disappointing to him is noticeable when in the conclusion of this admonition he graphically states what he believes:

"For there are many religious who, on the pretext of seeing something better than what their superiors order, look backward and return to the vomit of their selfwill. Such people are killers and cause many souls to be lost through their bad example" (Admonition 3).

These words may seem harsh in the mouth of the seraphic saint, but they were obviously inspired by his solicitude for his brothers. All these admonitions, however, remained without the desired effect. Indeed, in the year 1220, after Brother John a Capella, one of the original twelve, had dissociated himself from the Order and wanted to found a new community, Pope Honorius III, very probably at the petition of St. Francis himself, wrote a letter which made it possible to proceed with ecclesiastical punishment against such vagabond friars. This was repeated again in 1223. But with the loose structure of the Order at that time, it was ineffective. Francis was forced by the actual situation to formulate his conception of obedience more and more precisely and sharply until it was expressed in the image of the corpse — an image in which there is little left of the original idealism and chivalrous liberty of the early days.

By examining and reflecting on these words of the Testament we gained an insight into the beginnings of the Franciscan movement, an insight which in many respects is very instructive. Let us try, therefore, in conclusion, to draw from this brief summary what remains of lasting value for us:

1. Our look into the early Franciscan history has shown us that even then, when St. Francis himself was still living in the community, not everything was rosy. Even a saint like Francis had to fight against the all-too-human element in his young com-

munity. Because of the actual reality which the rapid growth of the Order brought about, he also had to undergo experiences disappointing to him and his idealism. But he did not capitulate. Nor did he venture into the romantic enthusiasm conjured up one hundred years later in the book of the "Fioretti." No, Francis objectively took into account reality and real people, as they are.

Therefore, he throws up a strong bulwark against any egoistic arbitrary action of man burdened by original sin. He becomes ever more conscious of the fact that no religious community can exist without the unifying bond of obedience, and this experience finds its concrete expression precisely in parts IX and X of his Testament.

I think it is quite evident that we do not need to pass through such experiments again today to reach the same conclusions as Francis in the end. We might indeed learn from history. But people always want to have the experience themselves, even if so much is destroyed by this — unfortunately!

2. This answers another question which results from meditation on the Testament. No doubt Francis also speaks in his spiritual testament about poverty, but only sporadically in connection with other questions. Still one might ask why there is no special section to inculcate poverty with this same insistence; why in his Testament, in this last message of St. Francis to his brothers, this strong and hard emphasis on obedience? Of course, we might rightly answer because it was especially necessary at that time. But if we consider the fact that in the writings of Francis handed down to us, the admonitions to obedience reach almost twice the number of those on poverty, in fact almost 2/3, then we might be puzzled after all. Does not poverty, according to general estimation, have primacy and precedence for Francis? Surely, but — and this we have in the course of history forgotten to a large extent — in the eyes of Francis obedience is an intrinsic element of poverty which is not exhausted by being poor in earthly things.

Thus Francis says in the third admonition when he explains the invitation of Christ:

"That person gives up everything he possesses and loses body and life, who keeps himself altogether ready for obedience at the hands of his superior . . ."

And in another place:

"He has not left everything for the sake of the Lord who still holds on to the purse of self-will" (2 C 140).

He is like Judas who did not follow the Lord unconditionally, but rather pursued his own will on the side and thus ended in destruction.

3. To give up everything for the Lord! Maybe it is not by accident that we find in this section motivation for our obedience to the superior "because he is my lord." Just as in part III Francis calls even sinful priests "his lords" in whom he does not want to consider their sin because he sees in them God's Son, here also Francis places obedience in the light of faith. To live in obedience means largely to live in faith and is only possible in faith; moreover, as the references to the life of Christ indicate again and again, to live in that faith which is also ready to make sacrifices, ready to sacrifice oneself for the sake of one's brothers.

Here we should ask ourselves when we speak about a crisis in obedience today if there is not behind this a crisis of faith, and if before praying for a life in obedience we should not ask for an increase in faith so that starting from a deep and firm faith we may reach a faith-filled obedience as Francis puts it before our eyes.

4. The obedient person makes such sacrifices in faith because he knows that only from this true community will grow. The disobedient person, however, considers his own interests higher than those of the community; as Francis expresses it very clearly, "he separates himself from the brothers." This can happen externally in many ways; but it doesn't happen only externally — it may also be done internally. Such a separation, however, such an aloofness from the community means a separation from the brothers, separation from the community — and this leads to the ruin of fraternal community life.

Those, however, who for the sake of all, are ready to make sacrifices to live in that real and loving obedience about which Francis says it is "to God's pleasure and the salvation of the neighbor," for those is the blessing of St. Francis:

"And if you observe the commandments of the Lord and what you have promised according to the holy gospel and your way of life, know that you are truly obedient and blessed by the Lord."

We are facing today all kinds of difficulties everywhere in religious life, in the Church. Would it not be salutary to call to mind again the vision of faith of St. Francis, so that we also and our communities may live in true obedience and be blessed by the Lord.

Almighty, holy God,
awaken in us that spirit
which moved your confessor and our holy Father, Francis,
so that we may be filled with the same spirit,
rejoice in meditating on what he has taught,
and seek to put it into practice,
through Christ our Lord. Amen.

XI

THE DIVINE OFFICE
(Sections 9 & 10 cont'd)

As we have seen, sections 9 and 10 of the Testament form an intrinsic unity. We first considered the topic of obedience, which is no doubt the most important in this section. Today we will consider the second topic, the praying of the Divine Office in community.

Let us first of all see what is written in the Testament on this point:

"And though I am simple and ailing I wish always to have a cleric who may recite the Office with me, as it is prescribed in the Rule (Testament, 9).

"And all the other friars are to be bound in like manner . . . to say the Office in the manner prescribed by the Rule" (Testament, 10).

Let us halt here. The following severe regulation against those who do not say the Office according to the Rule will be treated in the second part of this conference.

Our first question will be: what is the meaning of the words of Francis, "to say the Office according to the Rule?" The praying of the Office went through a great evolution in the growing community of Francis. Mainly this was just the result of circumstances.

In the beginning, as the biographers tell us, when they did not yet have the books needed for choir Office, the brothers prayed a number of Our Fathers or made a meditation at the different hours of the Office. The first biographer, Brother Thomas of Celano, moreover relates that, inflamed by the fire of the Holy Spirit, they even sang those Our Fathers.

This custom of praying the Our Father may seem somewhat strange to us, but in those days it was a general practice. Whoever was unable to read according to the meaning of the word in those days, — i.e., whoever was not a cleric, and this applied to men and women alike, therefore, whoever was not a scholar or an educated person, — or whoever was on a journey and therefore unable to take part in the common choir prayer, such persons prayed the Our Fathers because in those days there existed no breviaries as we know them now. Thus those who were traveling and could not assist at the Office, and those who could not read, said the prayer which every Christian knew: the Our Father; in this way they joined in the common prayer of the community and, beyond this, of the whole Church.

Here I would like to point out something interesting: the lay brothers prayed the Our Fathers. Formerly, when we still had the rosary, the rosary consisted of seven decades and six large beads; that was precisely the 76 Our Fathers which our lay brothers had to pray daily instead of the Office. The Dominicans had a rosary with 150 beads from which developed the other rosary, the one with the Hail Mary's. These were, therefore, strings of beads on which the lay brothers could count the number of Our Fathers and so say their Office. Later on the lay brothers did not pray this Our Father-office anymore, but those who prayed the breviary said the lay office, the rosary, besides. For lay people they made an even smaller Office, namely, the Angelus. And so the "obligation" remains for all of us even today, unless we have meantime liberated ourselves from it. One can also overdo it.

After the reform of the breviary under Innocent III, at the time of Francis, when there were real breviaries available, Francis imposed the obligation upon the clerics to say the Office as it was customary among the clergy of the Church of Rome. The lay brothers should continue to say for each hour a determined number of Our Fathers. Here, however, as we can already see in the number 76 versus 150, Francis remained far behind the measure which was customary in those days. Maybe he wanted to give the brothers the possibility of praying the Our Father-office in a more meditative way. The prescription in the Rule reads:

"Let the clerics say the Divine Office according to the custom of the holy Roman Church, excepting the Psalter; for that reason they may have breviaries. The lay brothers shall say 24 Our Fathers for the Matin, five for the Lauds, seven each for Prime, Tierce, Sext and None, for the Vespers twelve, and seven for the Compline" (II Rule 3).

This was also taken over by Clare in her rule and consequently the Sisters who were able to read said the breviary of the Friars Minor and the other Sisters the Our Father-office. But Clare added:

"And the sisters who for reasonable cause at times may not be able to say their Hours by reading them, may say the Our Father like other sisters" (Poor Clares Rule, 3).

From this, through the principle of communication of privileges, all Franciscan families enjoy this privilege: that for a good reason both Offices may be interchanged for they have similar prescriptions in their rules. This is still provided although the sisters are able to read nowadays. May I add here a personal remark? When I am traveling by train and the compartment is filled with people, I prefer to say my Our Father-office quietly instead of using the big book. One can also say it in a meditative way, especially if the journey is long.

I do not think we should lightly give up this precept of the 4th chapter of the Rule of the Third Order Regular. While traveling or in days of sickness or of vacation one can more easily switch over to the other Office.

To all his followers, however, Francis gave this exhortation which is valid for all times:

"In that love which is God, I entreat all my friars, ministers and subjects, to put away every attachment, all care and solicitude, and serve, love, honor and adore our Lord and God with a pure heart and mind; this is what he seeks above all else. . . . It is such men as these the Father claims for his worshippers . . . God is spirit, and they who worship him must worship in spirit and truth" (I Rule 23).

But the decisive sentence is this:

"Watch then, praying at all times . . . When you stand up to pray, say Our Father who art in heaven" (I Rule 23).

We must pray continually, never ceasing. These simple words reveal to us precisely how much Francis valued the Office which was prayed by day and by night. This appreciation we find also in the still more plain and simple words of the Testament:

"And though I am simple and ailing, I wish always to have a cleric who may recite the Office with me, as it is prescribed in the Rule" (Testament 9).

Here we can see that Francis did not want to renounce *praying the Office,* no matter what the cost.

But in these words something else also appears: Francis does not want to renounce praying the Office *in community.* Obviously he also wants the text of the Rule to be understood in this way — and thus the Order has understood him throughout its history. Even in times of sickness he wanted to pray the Office in common with another brother. This was taken as a matter of course at that time because choir books and breviaries were a rarity; they had to be copied by hand on parchment. All of you are familiar with the precious breviary of San Damiano of Assisi, this beautifully hand-written breviary lying in the reliquary; what a work, to copy such a book in such beautiful script on parchment! Therefore, it is understandable that not everyone could have a breviary; ordinarily there was one single copy and everyone knew the psalms by heart.

Besides this more obvious reason, the Church of the early centuries and of the Middle Ages had another reason for the common recitation of the Office. They were still very conscious of the fact that the Divine Office was prayed, as they said, "in persona

Ecclesiae," in the person of the Church. This means not only by order of the Church, or by mandate of the Church, but *in the name of the entire Church.*

The Church should be represented in this prayer by its delegates. This, however, could be meaningfully fulfilled and experienced only when it was done in common; for this reason the brothers prayed the Office in community. This was the explicit will of Francis, as testified by Thomas of Celano. Because the psalms are prayed in the choir "before the face of the angels," Francis wanted all the brothers who could do so, to come together in the oratory and pray the psalms attentively. Before the brothers had oratories of their own, they went to the churches in the neighborhood to pray the Office with the clergy there. In regard to this point Brother Jordan of Ciano relates a precious example from the early days of the Order in Germany. At the first provincial chapter in Worms in 1222, the brothers could not celebrate the Office together in their restricted quarters, so they convinced the bishop and the canons of the cathedral that they should be content with one side of the choir and leave the other side to the brothers. One side of the choir vied with the other in singing, relates Brother Jordan, and thus they said the Divine Office with great solemnity.

This must have been at the time of which Francis speaks in section IV of his Testament: "The clerics among us prayed the Office like other clerics," but as far as possible, as we can see, in common. This, however, does not exhaust the significance of the statement in the Testament. We must consider still another phrase:

"And should some be found who are not saying the Office according to the prescription of the Rule but are trying to introduce some other form of it, or who are not Catholics, . . ."

The connection here may seem unintelligible to us. What is the relation between this or that form of the Office and being Catholic? Here we must reach back again to the historical facts. At the time of St. Francis there raged in the Catholic Church of the West the heresy of the so-called Cathari. They believed in a good

God who had created the spiritual world and an evil God who had created the material world; the first was the God of the New Testament and the second of the Old Testament. In this way they gave a simple explanation for the problem of evil and suffering; these were attributed to the evil God who constantly tried to hinder the action of the good God. For this reason the radical Cathari, who were most strongly represented in central Italy, radically rejected the Old Testament. Since the Office of the Church consisted to a large extent of the words of the Old Testament and mainly of the psalms, they also radically rejected this form of prayer. Other Cathari accepted some parts and rejected others. It was, ultimately, as a protection against the evil of heresy that Francis accepted the Office of the Church of Rome. Moreover it was reported in this way by Angelus Clarenus who was not exactly friendly disposed toward Rome.

Obviously there were among the Friars Minor some who succumbed to the influence of Cathari ideas — modern in those times. Therefore Francis wrote already in his earlier Rule these words which may seem strange to us written into the Rule of an Order:

"All the brothers shall be Catholic and live and speak like Catholics. Should anyone, however, stray from the Catholic faith and life in speech or fact, and not amend, he should be expelled from our brotherhood" (I Rule 19).

Already in his letter to a General Chapter and All the Friars, Francis speaks equally as sternly as in his Testament.

"If any of the brothers refuse to observe these particulars, I do not regard them as Catholics or as my brothers, and I do not want to see or speak with them until they repent of it."

We see here also how alert Francis remains to the ecclesiastical life of his time. He knows that under the disguise of piety, heresy and division may creep into the fraternity and into the whole Church. There he is, as Julian of Speyer sings in the first line of his rhymed office of St. Francis, the totally Catholic man who stands radically for the faith but equally radically for the prayer of the Church of Rome.

Do I overstate my point? I don't think so. We should remember that in those days almost every diocese and religious Order had its own Office or Prayer of the Hours. Even the Dominicans, the Order of Friars Preachers, which was founded about the same time as the Friars Minor, developed its own liturgy of the Mass and of the Office. Francis could have done quite the same; it would have been nothing spectacular. But he did not do this; instead he took over for his Order, as we have seen, the Office and the liturgy of the Church of Rome. It was precisely in these essential elements of his fraternity that Francis wanted to be united with the Church in common prayer. This unconditional and unlimited fidelity in faith and prayer with the Catholic Church, Francis kept until his death. It was this fidelity that made him dictate into his Testament these words which we might deem harsh or perhaps exaggerated, which perhaps reveal a totally unfamiliar aspect of Francis, words which, however, because they are in the Testament, we must consider and will no doubt better understand:

"And should some be found who are not saying the Office according to the prescript of the Rule but are trying to introduce some other form of it, or who are not Catholic, all the friars, wherever they are, are to be bound in obedience to present any such, wherever they may find him, to the custos nearest the place where they have found him. And the custos is to be firmly bound by obedience to guard him day and night as a prisoner, so that he cannot escape his hands, until he shall in his own person deliver him into the hands of his minister. And the minister is to be firmly bound by obedience to send him by such friars who will day and night guard him as a prisoner until they bring him before the Lord of Ostia, who is the master of this whole brotherhood and has it under his protection and correction" (Testament 10).

Here we might ask: Are these really the words of the seraphic saint? Words of the man who would not harm any little animal? Words of the man who once gave a superior of the brothers this golden admonition of seraphic love:

"And I will take this as proof of whether you love the Lord and me, his servant and yours, if you act as follows: namely, that there be no brother in the world who has sinned as much as ever he could sin, yet who, after looking in your eyes, would ever go away without mercy from you if he seeks mercy, and if he were not to seek mercy you would ask him if he wished for mercy. And if he appeared before your eyes after that a thousand times, love him more than me, to the end that you may drag him to the Lord, and may you ever have pity on such persons (Letter to a Certain Minister).

When we compare both texts we ask ourselves if there could be a greater, a stronger contradiction?

But we should once more be clear on what we have just heard from the first Rule:

"Should anyone, however, stray from the Catholic faith and life in speech or fact, and not amend, he should be expelled from the brotherhood" (I Rule, 19).

Or the other word which we heard from the letter to the General Chapter:

"If any of the brothers refuse to observe these particulars (concerning the praying of the Office), I do not regard them as Catholics or as my brothers, and I do not want to see or speak with them until they repent of it."

It is obvious that whenever there is a question about the brothers being Catholic, Francis is inexorably hard. One can say that toward the end of his life he became increasingly severe, apparently because of the experiences he had to go through. But in all this Francis was faithful to what he had promised, with all its consequences, at the beginning of his religious life:

"Let Brother Francis and whoever will be the head of this Order promise obedience and reverence to the Lord Pope Innocent and his successors" (I Rule).

"Brother Francis promises obedience and reverence to the Lord Pope Honorius and his successors canonically entering office, and to the Roman Church" (II Rule).

Wherever this promise was in danger, be it in faith, in life style, or in prayer, there in the eyes of Francis the existence of his brotherhood, of the Franciscan movement, was at stake. And then there was for him only a decisive "no."

There are today no more Cathari or Waldensians who, under the guise of piety or apostolic life threaten to undermine the life of the Church from within and to destroy the unity of the Church. But if we are aware of the life of the Church in our days, as clearly alert as Francis was to the life of the Church in his time, we will know that today there are also disguises under which the powers against God want to invade the Church. We know also that these disguised evil powers do not halt before the community of St. Francis.

If, according to the word of Reinhold Schneider, "today is the hour of St. Francis," then it is the hour of confirmation of our Catholicity. Therefore each one of us should ask ourselves again and again whether we stand for what we promised on the day of our profession: to be obedient to the Lord Pope and to the Roman Church. Are we, in all the ecclesiastical discussions of our times, ready to follow constantly the footsteps of our Mother the Church with special dedication as Francis requires of his brothers? Do we have the courage to remain unflinchingly Catholic in the midst of the pietism and pietistic manifestations of our times?

Francis remained undisturbed and held to the truth. He remained within the Church.

If we look back on the text of the Testament which we considered together today we will come to the conclusion that in these inexorably hard-sounding words that which mattered after all was love — love for our Mother the Church outside of which, in the eyes of Francis, there is no salvation. But this love, endangered then as now, will not be realized somewhere in the air, but concretely, namely, in praying with the Church. Therefore these words reveal to us the love of our holy father Francis towards the unity of the Church. He does not tolerate any separation through subjective arbitrariness. He recognizes precisely in this essential element of religious life — in prayer — an order to which man must submit. He wants all his followers to serve this union with the Church in obedience and reverence. He decrees sanctions, as did Christ in Mt. 18:17: "If he does not listen to the church, be he to you like a pagan or sinner," that is, like a man who has excluded himself; so Francis also recognized this exclusion if they did not want to mend their ways.

In the same way St. Paul in I Cor. 5 expelled from the life of the Church the man who had given such great scandal in the community in order that his spirit might find salvation in the day of the Lord. Thus Francis also expels from the community those brothers who did not want to be Catholic, until they changed their minds.

We see, therefore, that Francis, also in this section of his testament, is completely in line with the New Testament when he loves the unity of the Church above all else. Could our attitude toward our Mother Church be any different?

On the other hand, the love of Francis for the prayer of the Church stands out clearly in these texts; precisely in prayer the Church should be one. This had Francis, the man of simple faith, understood when he bound his brothers so stringently with the prayer of the Church of Rome. In its cult the Church fulfills her highest and most important duty. In her worship she takes part in the high-priestly ministry of Jesus Christ; therefore, it is a grace for us to pray with the Church. It is our special vocation to pray as the Church.

We should deem ourselves fortunate to pray with Christ and in Him for the Church. Then can Francis consider us also as Catholics, as his true brothers and sisters, who do not let themselves be disconcerted or confused by anything or anyone, but like him, remain totally Catholic in the Church.

XII

OBSERVANCE OF THE RULE
(Section 11)

The next section of the Testament of St. Francis which we will consider is really short, but, it seems to me, very instructive in many respects. Before examining its meaning in detail, let us listen to the whole text:

"And the friars should not say: 'This is another Rule,' because this is a reminder of our past, an admonition and exhortation, and my testament, which I, the little Brother Francis, am making for you, my blest brothers, to this end, that we may observe in a more Catholic manner the Rule we have promised the Lord."

If we think again of sections IX and X which immediately precede this, the question which we would like to ask first is: where is the connection between section X with its severe punishments for those brothers who would not be Catholic, and this section XI? The question is fully justified. It is something which we should always ask when we read texts like this, because it will help us to penetrate more deeply into their meaning. This question also leads us to an examination of how Francis really thought. It will teach us to understand his writings better.

The whole text of the Testament gives us a convincing illustration of the way in which Francis used to talk and write. He refers to himself as ignorant and uneducated and in section IV of the Testament he calls himself and his brothers "simple and without learning." What he wants to say is that they had not attended special schools. They were simple people and therefore also simple in their manner of thinking. Francis did not think strictly logically as such, that is, following a strict train of thought — something like the way in which we had to write our compositions at school, where each point should always flow from the preceding one according to the rules of strict logic, otherwise the teacher would draw a line in the margin with the remark, "logical sequence?".

Francis thinks like all simple people — by association, i.e., more in images. His way of thinking is determined by concrete perceptual representations more than by strict logic of thought. There is more sparkling life and less bleak thought. Images and representations from life determine the train of thought. Let us clarify this by an example from the Testament because this also belongs to an understanding of Francis.

In section I, Francis relates how the Lord led him to a change in life, to conversion. This he makes clear by the example of his meeting with the leper. This short narration concludes with the brief sentence: "And then I tarried but a little while, and left the world." How did this come about; what did he do to carry out this resolution? We all know — he first devoted himself to repairing churches, because he had taken the mandate of the Crucified in its full literal meaning.

And then — for us rather abruptly — section II of the Testament continues, "And the Lord gave me such a faith in the churches . . ." These, however, are not only the churches he should repair but, as St. Bonaventure testifies, Francis learned to apply the words of the Crucified of San Damiano, "Go and repair my house," to that Church which Christ had bought with his blood. Of this Church, therefore, Francis also speaks in the short prayer in section II of the Testament, "We adore thee, Lord Jesus Christ . . ." The image of the Church always stands alive and concretely before Francis' eyes.

It is of this Church which comprises all the redeemed that he speaks in section III. He first sees her concretely, practically, in the priests who live according to the form of the holy Roman Church. He sees her very concretely as the Mother, the one who dispenses and preserves the Holy Eucharist, who teaches the true faith, who provides spirit and life. He not only sees her as such, but he thanks the Lord who grants it to him to encounter the Church with such faith. This is the end of the first series of thoughts.

With section IV there begins a new sequence of images which Francis recalls as he looks back on his life. He sees how the Lord leads brothers to him; how he finds in the Gospel for himself and his brothers their first rule of life; how the Lord Pope confirmed it. He sees how the brothers put Gospel poverty into practice; how they pray; how on their wanderings they pass the night in the churches. "And we were . . . subject to all," that is ready to serve. This was done by the brothers when they helped people in their work, when they gave their service to others.

Then follows immediately section V on the work of the brothers. They shall live from the work of their hands and only in case of need shall they beg: ". . . then let us have recourse to the table of the Lord and beg alms from door to door."

"From door to door" — this then is the occasion to speak in section VI of the greeting which the Lord revealed to him: "The Lord give you peace!"

Now Francis has lost himself completely in thoughts about the past. He saw how his brothers carried out their apostolate of wandering workmen and preachers. Then he remembers the present which should be so much different. The number of the brothers increases; they dwell in modest houses and they also have small churches. Francis is not against this development. He sees its necessity.

But in section VII he indicates the spirit which should animate everything, the spirit of poverty, the spirit of pilgrimage which has no permanent dwelling. This spirit must be preserved in everything.

Therefore, in section VIII he forbids the acceptance of papal letters of protection for churches and houses, for body and life. This series of thoughts ends with the indication that the life of penance according to the Gospel can be led always and everywhere and in all countries. Thus this sequence of thoughts comes to a close.

With section IX there begins a new series of representations. The great number of brothers spread throughout all countries, threatened by the prevailing heresy of that time, needed a strong control. This control Francis saw more and more in obedience and, for that time — maybe also for our time again — in the liturgy of the Church. He speaks of both in sections IX and X, ending with the stern penalty for those brothers "who are not Catholic." They should be taken to the Cardinal of Ostia who should be the protector of the whole fraternity. At the end of this section, Francis sees then before his eyes the living figure of the Cardinal of Ostia to whom those brothers who became heretical must be led. It is this figure which leads the train of thought into section XI, which to us seemed so erratic at the beginning. Why?

In the course of the preceding exposition, Francis not only gave advice but also orders of obedience in the strict sense:

"The friars should make sure . . ."

"I firmly command all the friars by obedience that wherever they may be . . ."

"And all other friars are to be bound . . ."

"And the custos is to be firmly bound by obedience . . ."

In his Testament Francis has in reality added some strongly obligating commands to the text of the Rule. He wanted to do the same on another occasion, as Thomas of Celano relates, but then he was forbidden to do so because the approbation of the Rule already given by the Pope did not allow it anymore. If, therefore, we ask for a transition from section X to section XI, it will be nothing but the warning finger of the Lord Cardinal of Ostia.

Suddenly Francis remembers that "What I have done I can't do at all in this manner." So, what does he do then? Now we can understand the following section XI.

"The brothers should not say, 'This is another Rule,' because this is a reminder of our past, an admonition and exhortation" — notwithstanding all the commands under obedience!

In this way Francis on the one hand wants to do justice to the Cardinal, but on the other hand he wants to save his parting words to the brothers. He was, and this we feel very strongly here, neither a lawyer nor a canonist. Therefore, in order to resolve the doubts of conscience of many brothers, the Lord of Ostia, after he became Pope Gregory IX, declared solemnly that they were not bound *in conscience* to observe the Testament. The Lord Cardinal was namely a lawyer and resolved the case strictly juridically.

But the very little Francis, who called himself uneducated but who was not really that stupid after all, had almost clairvoyantly taken precautions against this by speaking not only of a reminder, an admonition and an exhortation but by calling this last writing his "Testament." The word testament, of course, should not be understood here in its juridical sense, as a last will of binding disposition concerning possessions and property, but as a spiritual document, as a sign of his memory and his blessing and of their covenant, their unitedness, which should bind him with his brothers in one will even beyond death. It should be a word from brother to brother along the way to God. Francis had thought, as always, of those who were now in the Order and those who would enter the Order until the end of the world. All these should form with him a community of spirit, a union of like-minded persons. Let us remember that "testamentum" in Latin can mean a written document, but at the same time, it can mean the bond into which one enters, just as we still speak about the Old Testament and the New Testament, the Old Covenant and the New Covenant. Francis therefore, considers the community of those who will follow him as covenanted people, a bonding before God of people who are united in the same spirit.

And therefore, he, the very little, unimportant Brother Francis, suddenly turns to those addressed by the document:

". . . which I am making for you, my blest brothers."

A wonderful word: "You, my blest brothers!" — one which

Francis often uses when he speaks about or to his brothers. It can be translated in different ways: "You, my blest brothers," meaning certainly, you, my brothers blest by God; but it can also mean, you, my brothers approved by God, i.e., loved by God, called by God, affirmed by God; you, my brothers, who are standing in the blessing of God who loves you. What great reverence is spoken by these words written by a plain, simple man.

How much would not this — to pause here a moment — change our mutual human relationships if we always remained conscious of this reality — that we are brothers and sisters blest by God, approved by God, affirmed by God and loved by God. Such a word could bring about a revolution in a community, but a revolution in the sense of the Gospel.

Francis is so deeply convinced of the dignity of his brothers before God, that he calls himself their "frater Franciscus parvulus." Behind this word we recognize without difficulty the Italian "Frate Francesco piccolo" (Little Brother Francis) — the origin of this community, but he is also its head, its leader, its highest superior. He does not see the brothers in themselves, nor in relation to himself, but he sees the brothers in the loving grace of God. He sees them so exalted in the affirming blessing of God, that he knows himself to be the very little one, the most unimportant one. Here we perceive, from these very simple words, what humility animated this man. His faith-vision of the brothers changes for him, again, all mutual human relationships: my behavior toward another is not determined by my judgment of him, but by God's judgment of him. God, however, has called him not only as a Christian but, still more, into this community. God blesses him; God gives himself to him day after day; therefore God must love him immensely. These are "my blest brothers" and sisters and therefore I must esteem these others, treat them with reverence, I — the very little one, the most unimportant one — and these others, they are loved by God, indeed blest by Him.

In this interpretation is revealed the foundation of that bond which will bind Francis to all those who want to follow him until the end of the world: the respectful esteem and the loving humility of all toward all, because God has chosen them and called them.

And once more Francis, in holy simplicity, anticipates the juridical decision of Gregory IX by saying that he does not want to place a new Rule against the only valid one approved by the Pope, but that he wrote the Testament —

". . . to this end, that we may observe in a more Catholic manner the Rule we have promised the Lord."

First of all, a linguistic peculiarity should be pointed out here. Francis does not say "which *I* write for *you* in order that *you* may observe the Rule which *you* have promised the Lord." No, he does not speak as from superior to subject. He includes himself in the bond in which they have united themselves by their religious profession. He includes himself in this bond as one who could serve God more faithfully, "in a more Catholic manner." It is an echo of the word he once spoke to the brothers near the end of his days, "Brothers, let us begin now to serve God, the Lord, because until now we have hardly made any progress at all."

Therefore, Francis considers his Testament as an admonition, an exhortation also for himself. As so often before, we see here again that Francis never admonishes others without admonishing himself; he does not oblige others to things which he is not ready to do himself. Let us remember here section V: "And I was wont to work with my hands . . . and I earnestly wish that all the friars be occupied with some kind of work." Or sections IX and X: "And it is my firm desire to obey" and to "recite the Office . . . and all the other friars are to be bound in like manner to obey their guardians and to say the Office in the manner prescribed by the Rule."

We can also add from his Testament to the Sisters of St. Clare:

"I, little Brother Francis, wish to live according to the life and poverty of our most high Lord Jesus Christ and his most holy Mother and to persevere in this to the last. And I beseech you, my Ladies, and I exhort you to live always in this most holy life and poverty."

It is always a matter of "we," so that all of us, superiors and subjects, the first and the last, the last and the first, conform in our whole life to what we have promised the Lord to observe.

To continue our thought, there is no question of opposition between the Rule and the Testament, about which we read so many arguments in the well known book of Fr. von Galli, S.J., as if the Testament were a unique flaming protest against the Rule which the learned brothers with the help of the Roman Curia extorted from him; as if, therefore, the Testament were an attempt by Francis to free himself of every learned and curial tutelage which had diluted his ideals.

The Dutch Fr. Fidentius van den Borne once spoke in this connection of a drama which never took place. But how boring would not our biographies of St. Francis be if one could not repeatedly touch up this drama of the first one to counteract, of one who rebelled, precisely in his Testament! All this flounders before the simple words of Francis himself when we read, "that we may observe in a more Catholic manner the Rule we have promised the Lord." And is it not so in the whole of the Testament? The heretics of that time rejected the Church, the churches as places of prayer; Francis restores them and he believes in the mystery present in them (section II).

The heretics of those times rejected the priesthood and asserted that a good lay person could do more than a bad priest; ordination is of no importance. Francis honors the priests as his lords because of their ordination, even if they are sinners (section IIIa).

The Cathari in those days rejected the Holy Eucharist as deviltry. Tepid Christians trampled upon It — literally. Francis, in reverent faith, wants to keep It in precious places and to honor and adore It above everything (section IIIb). Many heretical teachers at that time rejected the Old Testament and wanted to hear nothing of theology. Francis venerates God's word and those who explain it to us (section IIIb).

Many in those times wanted to lead a life according to the Gospel, an apostolic life, but they disagreed with the Church and its pastoral role. Francis wants to follow God's revelation in his way of life but only with the approval of the Lord Pope, as we heard in section IV: "The most High himself revealed (it) to me . . . and the Lord Pope confirmed it to me."

Many in those days rejected the canonical prayer of the Hours and the sacred liturgy in general. Francis wants to keep them firmly and never break away from the communion of prayer with the Church, as we heard in sections IX and X.

Yet, it is truly so that Francis wrote the Testament in order that we may observe the Rule in a Catholic fashion — not as a manifestation well planned, not as a program clearly stylized; no, it gushes forth freely from heart to heart. And this is really the deepest meaning of this document, which for us also has not lost its significance even though perhaps many things are different today.

Wherever the life of the Church is attacked or injured, Francis does not oppose, he does not judge or condemn anything or anyone; he does but one thing: he stands up with greater faith and living love — and to this he would like to lead also all those whom God gives him.

It is up to us to recognize the signs of our time so that we in our time, in our surroundings, "observe in a more Catholic manner the Rule we have promised the Lord." And even if today the doctrine and the life of the Church is perhaps not threatened by manifest heresies, still many things happen which we cannot approve. And here we should learn from Francis not to complain about those who are too conservative or too progressive, about this or that tendency, but to do the right thing with greater faith and more lively love so "that we may observe in a more Catholic manner the Rule we have promised the Lord."

> Most holy and glorious God,
> enlighten the darkness of my heart
> and grant me genuine faith,
> firm hope and perfect love.
> Give me, O Lord,
> true perception and understanding
> so that I may fulfill the holy mandate
> which in truth you have given me.

XIII

NO GLOSS OR ADDITION
(Section 12)

It is evident that, in the two sections XI and XII which conclude the presentation of the Testament, the central point is the concern of Francis for the Rule of the Order. This was already clear last time when we considered together Section XI. We felt how concerned the saint was that the brothers might observe the Rule "in a more Catholic manner," i.e., always in agreement with the doctrine and the life of the Catholic Church. The Rule, approved by the Church, should be the unifying bond of the fraternity. In his Testament Francis gives to this Rule what we would call in modern usage the first Constitutions. Therefore they together form the foundation on which the bond is built. This idea is further developed by Francis in section XII.

"And the Minister General and all other ministers and custodes shall be bound by obedience not to add to these words or take away from them. And let them always have this writing with them together with the Rule. And in all the Chapters they hold, when they read the Rule, let them read these words also. And all my brothers, both clerics and laics, I firmly charge by obedience not to make any explanation of the Rule or of these words and

197

say: 'Thus they are to be understood.' Rather, as the Lord has granted me simply and plainly to speak and write the Rule and these words, so simply and without gloss you are to understand them, and by holy deeds carry them out to the very end."

When we read or hear these words for the first time, unbiased, there surely arises immediately the question: Is this really Francis who is speaking? Is this really Francis, who placed his own life and that of his brothers so directly under God's action, who was in everything so anxious that God, who speaks and does all good, may be the free and unhindered guide of the life of the brotherhood? Does he not here fetter the development of his Order in such a way that it might hinder its future expansion and restrict its activity for the Church and the world? Are not these severe prohibitions which Francis pronounces here obsolete, particularly for us Franciscans who have been called by Vatican II to an adapted renovation of the life of the Order? If we consider the words of Pope Paul VI who said expressly: "Nevertheless, suitable renewal cannot be made once and for all but should be encouraged in a continuing way, with the help of the zeal of the members and the solicitude of the chapters and superiors" (Ecclesiae Sanctae, II, 19), should we not admit that the severe prohibitions of this section are overruled by the teaching and the life of the Church itself?

All these are serious questions which we cannot lightly brush aside. We could simply say that these words are not binding for us; that they do not contain any juridical obligation for us — as Pope Gregory IX himself already declared concerning this section — and that they do not bind us strictly in conscience. Then, of course, the problem would be solved and we could calmly conclude these our considerations.

But I don't believe this would satisfy us. Could we so lightly disregard this last will and admonition of our *Father* which he, in the face of death, left to his children, present and future? Would we not break the fidelity of children to their father if we took things so lightly?

The solution of these grave problems might be sought in a

distinction which we made several times already in the course of our considerations of the Testament. We must distinguish between the wording which came into existence historically and which then, when it came into being, had a very special meaning — what the exegetes today rightly call its "Sitz im Leben" (real life situation) — and its spiritual, timelessly valid meaning which is hidden in this timebound wording. This is a distinction which we should always make whenever we wish to understand rightly the revelation of God which became Word in Holy Scripture. St. Paul warned us once and for all: "The letter kills but the spirit gives life" (2 Cor 3:6).

Therefore, what we should state first of all is this: Francis here, as so often in his Testaament, reacts against some definite abuses in his fraternity. In the face of death, driven by his last solicitude and responsibility for his own, he reacts sharply, even one-sidedly. Let us but remember the position he took on obedience and the praying of the Office in sections IX and X. There we must understand many things from the moment in which Francis dictated his words. As we did in the question of obedience, we must place many things in the context of the whole teaching of the saint on this theme. We must not consider single words of his in isolation.

Let us therefore inquire about the situation in which Francis wrote these words. We know now that the last years of his life were painfully overshadowed by the experience that many of the brothers did not live as they had promised the Lord. Many of them remained far behind the lofty ideal which the Rule placed before their eyes' and to which they had obliged themselves by their profession before God and before the Church as the norm of their life. This may not necessarily have happened out of bad will. Many other reasons were added to this: as always and everywhere, human frailty, the weakness of man burdened by original sin whose ego never bows before God's will; furthermore the additional reasons of the fast growing number of brothers at which Francis himself shuddered; and the lack of appropriate formation resulting therefrom because the charism of Francis seldom and sometimes never reached the individual brothers.

The early days of the charismatically formed and easily reachable small groups was irrevocably gone, and Francis may have foreseen what his death would mean to the Order. Did he not say immediately before his death: "I have done my part; may Christ teach you what is yours" (2 Cel 214).

Let us also remember that the brothers only slowly became settled residents and therefore it was always possible that some went their own way when the superiors or the brothers did not suit them; the third admonition, in fact, describes this in a moving manner. Finally, there were those brothers who would have preferred to keep everything according to the Rivo Torto conditions and remain forever in their little hermitages while others saw the need of the Church threatened by heresies and felt themselves, as apostolic men, obliged to preserve the purity of the Gospel for the Christian people. Indeed, it was a situation filled with tensions in many respects and in the face of which the ministers, the persons responsible for the individual groups and for related groups called provinces, stood rather helpless. For what did they have at their service? A Rule which supplied more spirituality than concrete directives for daily life and life in community — and now the Testament, again a spiritual document which gave more spiritual directives than useful means for the daily difficulties.

Quite surely St. Francis saw all this. It filled him with deep concern. But here also he remained faithful to himself. Surely, looking at the externals, he gave a few strong prohibitions. But the Lord gave him also in these the opportunity to utter words of orientation for the future. To extract and to explain these will be the object of our further considerations.

"And the Minister General and all other ministers and custodes shall be bound by obedience not to add to these words or take away from them."

First of all it should be noted here that Francis uses expressions which already in the Old Testament characterize every covenant (cf. Dt. 4:2; 12:32; Prov. 30:6), and which are also used in the New Testament (Apoc 22:18). The document of the covenant is considered inviolable. It binds the leaders of the people in the same way as the people themselves. Francis considers himself along with his brothers as the new people of God, united and kept together by the Rule which should be supported by the Testament. Therefore he calls it not only "the book of life, the marrow of the Gospel, the hope of salvation," but also "the bond of the eternal covenant" (2 Cel 208). As such it is a fundamental law which forms an unalterable core. Add to this the fact that in the Middle Ages "life according to the Rule" made an Order into an Order and that through the profession of the Rule one became a member of an Order. But then the concrete life of the Friars Minor was so fundamentally different from religious life existing hitherto in the Church that Francis also, from this viewpoint, had to take care to preserve the purity of the "vita regularis," the life according to the Rule. We can understand his concern regarding this important point. Thus a stable, constant element is established as is needed in every human society and without which it would disintegrate.

"And let them always have this writing with them together with the Rule."

Why? Surely not as a kind of talisman or a kind of relic. Francis himself gives us the best explanation of this sentence to which really nothing need be added:

"He wanted it to be had by all, to be known by all, and he wanted it to speak everywhere to the interior man unto his comfort in weariness and unto a remembrance of the vows he had made. He taught them to keep it ever before their eyes as a reminder of the life they were to live, and, what is more, that they should die with it" (2 Cel 208).

Every single friar, every single sister, should therefore know the Rule and the Testament. They should surely not carry it with them externally as a written text, but carry it primarily in their hearts as the core of life which receives ever anew from these documents its form, its spirit and vitality, and which should always serve as a norm in any emerging perplexity.

"And in all the chapters they hold, when they read the Rule, let them read these words also."

Not only should the life of the single individual be shaped by the Rule, but also the life of the community. The communities should let themselves be formed by it and this primarily in the respective chapters. This was a fixed custom in the Order from the beginning; and Francis, as he himself testifies, always observed this custom. At the chapters the Rule was not only read but also discussed. The lives of the individuals as well as that of the community were examined in its light; unsuitable points were eliminated from the Rule, hazy points were explained, many things were made more complete and improved; a path toward the future was adopted. In short, even though the Rule and the Testament (today we would say: the Rule and the constitution) are the stable and constant elements of community life, they do not exist for themselves but in order to serve the life of the fraternity. In the chapters they were adapted to life. To do this was not the business of the individual but of the community which gathers for the chapter. In this way Francis gave the development of the Order a dynamic element. In the constantly renewed constitutions he always tried, according to the changing conditions of the times, to adapt the meaning and content of the Rule to these new circumstances. This is an unending task!

"And all my brothers, both clerics and laics, I firmly charge by obedience not to make any explanations of the Rule or of these words and say: 'Thus they are to be understood.' "

Here a clarifying word should be said first: if all of us were not suffering from the distorting effects of original sin we would not need a Rule or a constitution. The first and most important task of the Rule and the constitution is to curb the selfishness rooted in every person so that a bearable community life can be made possible. Let us remember again that Francis said the Rule should be an encouraging admonition to overcome our reluctance. Such moments of reluctance occur in the life of everyone; they also occur in the life of the community. Then the Rule and the constitution become a support to prevent a breakdown; they become a bond which holds together and preserves community.

At such times, however, there exists the danger, which Francis saw clearly, that in their self-centeredness single persons or groups try to explain the Rule and the constitution in the light of their selfishness, saying: It should be understood *like this*! Seen externally, they do not touch the existing order but they know very well how to interpret it to their own advantage. This is true not only for the so-called progressives but also for the conservatives! Each knows how to promote his own interests: As *I* think, so it should be understood! But this self-centeredness of individuals and groups will wreck Christian fraternity and life in community.

"Rather, as the Lord has granted me simply and plainly to speak and write the Rule and these words, so simply and without gloss you are to understand them, and by holy deeds carry them out to the very end."

Where human selfishness seeks to clarify things and conditions, everything becomes obscure and complicated. Then begins a time of endless discussions which bear little or no fruit. But where life and fraternity are considered plainly and clearly, with simplicity and faith, in the light of the order given by God, there the individual will serve the whole; there, with a sanctifying effect, he will observe everything which furthers community, at all times and in all things till the end. Selfishness causes dissension, obscurity and difficulties. The one who says yes to the order the Lord has given us, lives in the light and radiates light. Such a life will be fruitful and sanctifying before God and before all others.

Francis was not a sociologist nor an expert in social problems. Certainly he faced the problems of human relationships in all their harshness. But how did he solve these problems? Not with new laws and regulations, but with an urging appeal to our spiritual attitude: that we should live plainly, simply, and in the spirit of faith, the way of life which God has given us through the Church and to which we have bound ourselves by our religious profession. For, as Francis says,

"A man has only as much knowledge as he puts into practice" (Mirror of Perfection, 4).

Let us therefore pray with our Father St. Francis:

> O great God of glory,
> my Lord Jesus Christ,
> I entreat you,
> put light into the darkness of my mind.
> Give me the right faith,
> firm hope, and perfect charity.
> Help me learn to know you, O Lord,
> so well that in all things
> I may do everything
> in true keeping with your holy will.

XIV

BLESSING OF FRANCIS
(Section 13)

We now come to the closing section of the Testament of our Holy Father Francis, which in reality is but a great and solemn blessing. That is something worthy of note. Whoever reads the writings of Francis with attention will, perhaps with surprise, discover how he regarded as having God's special blessing all who accepted his words with a sincere heart, who were ready and willing to put them into practice and who observed them with holy intention.

In the conclusion of the first Rule for the community of the friars, which we have preserved, we read:

"I beg almighty God, Three and One, to bless those who teach, learn, or have by them this Rule, keeping it fresh in their memory and putting it into practice, as they repeat and perform what is written in it for our salvation. Prostrate at their feet, I beg them all to love, observe, and treasure this Rule" (Rule of 1221).

The words of blessing which conclude the letters from Francis are more brief, such as those at the end of the "Letter to a General Chapter," which is at the same time however addressed to the entire Order:

"May you who do this be blessed by God and may God be ever with you. Amen."

"You who do this" is precisely explained in the preceding paragraph:

"Through our Lord Jesus Christ, I, Brother Francis, worthless as I am and an unworthy creature of the Lord God, command Brother Elias, Minister General of the Order, and all his successors, with the other superiors and guardians, present and to come, to keep a copy of this letter and put it into practice, preserving it carefully. I beseech them to observe scrupulously all that is written in it and to see that it is observed by others, according to the good pleasure of Almighty God, now and forever, as long as the world lasts."

I believe that precisely in these words we experience for the first time something of the prophetic consciousness of Francis. On the one hand he is convinced of what he is when he says, "worthless as I am and an unworthy creature of the Lord;" on the other hand, he says, "through our Lord Jesus Christ," — not "in the name of" nor "by mandate of." No; "through our Lord Jesus Christ." Christ speaks through him as God spoke through the prophets. He is the messenger of Christ, the one who proclaims that which is "according to the good pleasure of almighty God." Out of this prophetic sense of mission Francis pronounces the blessing of God on all who act according to his words. The Lord is forever with them.

A new factor is revealed in the blessing at the close of the "Letter to All Superiors of the Friars Minor":

"My friars and superiors who receive this letter can be sure that they have God's blessing and mine, if they copy and keep it, and have copies made for the friars who are devoted to preaching or are superiors, and if they preach all that is contained in it to the last."

This is actually surprising to us if we think about how humble and simple this man usually is. But when it is a matter of salvation for others, then he knows he is supported by God, is commissioned by God, and that these words of his will in like manner be accepted by Him. We feel that he is not concerned as to whether the friars are willing to accept his words, carefully preserve them and observe them faithfully, but rather — and it was much more difficult at that time than it is now — that they copy them or have them copied so that his words might be passed on to others. But even that was not sufficient for him; the friars should further spread his words through their preaching to the Christian folk. If they did that, if they so entered into the service of the prophetic mission of Francis, then could they be assured that they had the blessing of God and of his servant, his messenger, his prophet, Francis.

Francis' "Letter to All Clerics" further gives evidence that this is not a matter of a one-time publication:

"Anyone who has this writing copied, so that it may be obeyed more widely, can be sure that he has God's blessing."

Perhaps Francis' sense of mission comes from his interpretation of the apostolic life to which belongs the proclamation of the Word of God, for he once said that preachers "have been chosen by a certain great king to deliver to the people the edicts that proceed from his mouth" (2 Cel 163). The prophetic mandate cannot be more beautifully described. There are persons chosen by God who receive the word from His hand in order to pass it on. I believe that this expression can serve well today to explain the term "prophetic." There are those who present themselves as prophets and proclaim their own opinions and not that which they have received from the mouth of God. Francis' writings give eloquent testimony to the fact that he never preached of himself or sought to convince another of his opinion. On the contrary, his writings indicate that he carried out whatever he exhorted others to do:

"The preacher must first draw from secret prayer what he will later pour out in holy sermons; he must first grow hot within before he speaks words that are in themselves cold" (2 Cel, 163).

Because Francis received all that he proclaimed, particularly in his writings, from the mouth of the great King who revealed it to him in the stillness of prayer, all those who accept his words, preserve them in ready and willing hearts, and live them out, "can be sure they have God's blessing" (Letter to All Superiors).

Francis comprehensively expressed this at the conclusion of each of the important communications which he sent to the first brothers and sisters of penance with whom he felt a special bond, as well as to those men and women from whose associations the Third Order developed. In his so-called "Letter to All the Faithful" he tried to interpret for them their life according to the spirit of the Gospel. He permeated it with the life of the Triune God and introduced the perfect life of the Christian. Like a true prophet, a man of the Spirit, he presented anew the teachings of the Gospel to his followers, the religiously animated circles of that time. Thus the letter concludes:

"In the name of the Father and of the Son and of the Holy Spirit. Amen. In that love which is God, I, Brother Francis, the least of your servants and worthy only to kiss your feet, beg and implore all those to whom this letter comes to hear these words of our Lord Jesus Christ in a spirit of humility and love, putting them into practice with all gentleness and observing them perfectly. Those who can not read should have them read to them often and keep them ever before their eyes, by persevering in doing good to the last, because they are spirit and life. Those who fail to do this shall be held to account for it before the judgment-seat of Christ at the last day. And may God, Father, Son, and Holy Spirit, bless those who welcome them and grasp them and send copies to others, if they persevere in them to the last."

With astounding humility Francis here returns to "these words of our Lord Jesus Christ" which he realizes he is called to proclaim.

"I, . . . the least of your servants and worthy only to kiss your feet."

He wills to make himself insignificant if only his followers will accept and live according to the Christian message. For the sake of the message he presents the possibility of judgment to them but, for those who remain faithful until the end, also the happiness of a life blessed by the Triune God, a life which will be transformed into communion with the Trinity and which is without end.

This paragraph at the conclusion of the "Letter to All the Faithful" shows us in particular a Francis that we otherwise could not know. It shows us Francis as a man who is completely absorbed in his mission, in his awareness that he is a chosen instrument, a creature-instrument — and thus his humility — but an instrument in the hand of God, and therefore his consciousness of being sent; therefore his earnest challenge to take his words seriously and to observe them faithfully. Here actually a bit of prophecy is being revealed to us.

All these benedictions of Francis are connected with that final one at the end of his Testament which he expressed after fulfilling the mission which God had given him and before taking leave of this earth. You know well this blessing because it is the one Pius XI placed at the end of the Rule for the Third Order Regular:

"And everyone that shall observe these things, may he be filled in heaven with the blessing of the most high Father; and may he be filled on earth with the blessing of his beloved Son in fellowship with the most Holy Spirit the Comforter and all the powers of heaven and all the Saints. And I, Brother Francis, your little servant, as much as I can, confirm to you within and without this most holy blessing."

Before we delve into the deep theological content of this blessing, let us try to comment on some concepts which can serve to deepen our understanding.

"And everyone that shall observe these things." In Latin the expression is *quicumque;* that is, whoever. No one is excluded because the message of the Gospel which Francis revived, is basically for all.

Whoever shall observe "these things," which spelled out means Rule and Testament; that is, however, according to the form of life of the Gospel which the Pope had approved for him and his friars. For us today that means the Rule of life given us by the Church. Therefore Pius XI placed this blessing of Francis, as

I have already mentioned, at the close of the revised Rule of the Third Order Regular.

In the course of the blessing "all the powers of heaven" are mentioned. Here Francis is surely thinking of "heaven and all the powers of heaven" with whom, according to the words of many Prefaces in the Eucharistic liturgy, we should sing the triple holy, holy, holy; that is, with the choirs of angels in heaven.

"As much as I can," should also be explained. The Latin here is *quatcumque*, as large as possible, as much as possible, as comprehensively as I can. Francis will keep nothing for himself. Everything that he had received in blessing he will without exception pass on to each and everyone whoever observed this. The poor Francis gave intact to all those of good intent the entire wealth of grace which he had received.

To see how Francis understood this in individual cases, let us repeat here his blessing of Brother Elias which he pronounced at almost the same time:

"I bless you, my son, in all and through all things . . . May God, the King of all things, bless you in heaven and on earth. I bless you as much as I can and more than I can, and what I have not the power to do, may He be able to do in you who can do all things. . . . May you find every blessing you desire, and may whatever you ask for worthily, be fulfilled" (I Cel, 108).

This definitely clarifies what Francis intends to say when he confirms this sacred blessing as much as possible and as comprehensively as he can, both "within and without."

Thus we come to the main point, the central question: what did Francis mean when he used the word "bless"? If we consider the works written in his own hand, then we can be certain that Francis, one would almost say consciously, always wrote the Latin word for blessing, *benedicere,* as two words in the Italian: *bene dire.* Then it must be translated as: well said, well spoken, good wishes, to wish well. If we think of the Italian word *benedire,* we can also translate it as: approved, to say of something that it is good, to affirm something as good. Thus when Francis said,

"May God bless you," he meant, "May God approve of you; may He say his 'well done,' his 'yes' to you."

Is there anything that could bring us greater happiness than Gods saying "yes" to our way of living? Than our being aware of this "yes" of recognition on the part of God? Than God's being able to say that our life is good, that He approves of it? Surely that would be the fullness of blessing! Blessed is the person in whom this is ratified.

But *benedire* also means that God imparts good things to us so that, since His word is never without effect, He brings about good in us and through us. By means of God's blessing we are brought into the stream of God's own goodness which proceeds from the Father in heaven, comes to the Son on earth and unites all that is in heaven and on earth in the Holy Spirit. May this divine Goodness fill everyone who contemplates this.

If we would consider the Rule in the light of this final blessing, would not much of it be read in a different light? First of all, there is the blessing of the Almighty Father who is in heaven, the source from whom all good things come; the source of all goodness which streams forth endlessly in overflowing fullness but never overwhelms; which fills without measure and yet makes possible further openness to receive. Whoever receives it, whoever is filled by it, lives within God's world and, even though not apparently, is already in heaven because the Father has said "yes" to him; He approves of him and his life.

Whoever lives the Gospel life and makes it more and more his own, will "be filled on earth with the blessing of His beloved Son," through whose incarnation, suffering and death, resurrection and ascension God's "yes" to us and for us here on earth was made visible, touchable and humanly tangible. In Christ the fullness of the divine blessing is granted us on earth. Whoever lives his life according to the Gospel is covered by this blessing, by the power of the saving and sanctifying suffering, death and resurrection of Christ. He lives, as Francis so plainly says in his Testament, "in fellowship with the most Holy Spirit the Comforter," He who is the fullness of love between Father and Son; He who unites and maintains the communion of the saints, the life of angels and saints, "all the powers of heaven." God Himself will be the constant source of blessing for us.

And this blessing from which nothing shall be excluded, "within and without," the humble Francis confirms, he who is a new patriarch for all who are called to follow him, a father with a new patrimonial blessing, for he is called at one and the same time to represent God and mandated to dispense his benediction. In this blessing he places his followers, those present and those to come, within the life and action of the Triune God. And with that he entrusts to Him the work which, at God's command, he accomplished among his own. With this blessing he returns to God, to a certain extent, that which he was able to accomplish on earth through this divine blessing.

To us, however, this blessing, which is capable of activating all — God in heaven; Christ in the Church on earth; the Holy Spirit within the Church; in heaven the angels and saints — shows how earnest St. Francis is regarding this blessing for all who are connected with his mission, with his charism, with the work given him by God. His great fatherly love, his prophetic sense of mission, his selfless humility radiate from these at once solemn and yet so simple words which reveal to us his goal more admirably than anything else could.

What better spiritual benefit can we wish for, what greater goal can we hope for in the Franciscan Order than that this blessing of St. Francis may fill each one of us so that we increasingly become and live in such a way that God can say his "bene," his "yes" to all that we do. Then will we be secure in his grace on earth and in heaven.

> Almighty, most holy,
> most high and sovereign God,
> the sovereign good,
> everything that is good, wholly good,
> who alone are good:

to you let us render all praise,
all glory, all thanks,
all honor, all blessing,
and to you let us refer always
whatever is good.

— *St. Francis of Assisi*

Appendix

I

MESSAGE OF ST. FRANCIS TO THE POOR CLARES OF SAN DAMIANO
(Discovered in Verona, October 5, 1976)

The day after the 750th anniversary of the death of St. Francis,
Padre Giovanni Boccali O.F.M., of Assisi, found in two medieval
manuscripts in Verona what may be "those holy words" which
St. Francis sent to the Poor Clares of San Damiano when he was
staying there in the chaplain's house seriously ill in 1225 (for the
circumstances and a digest of the Message, see Legend of Perugia
45 in Omnibus *p. 1024-25 or in Fr. Salvator Butler's* We Were
With St. Francis *p. 176; and* Mirror of Perfection *90 in* Omnibus
p. 1223-24). The two slightly different versions will be published,
with full analysis and commentary, by the Biblioteca Francescana,
Chiesa Nuova, Assisi. At present Padre Boccali is not prepared
to state positively that they are or are not by St. Francis or a
secretary or editor. In my amateur opinion, I believe that the
oldest of the two manuscript versions can be attributed to St.
Francis. Here is my literal translation of its Italian text:
Hear, little poor ones (*poverelle*) called by the Lord,
   Who from many parts and provinces have come together:

217

Live always in truth,
>   So that in obedience you die.
Do not look to the life outside,
>   For that of the Spirit is better.
I pray you with great love
>>   That you have discretion as to the alms
>>   Which the Lord gives you.
Those who are weighed down by infirmities
>>   And the others who labor for them,
>>   All of you bear it in peace,
>>   For you will see this labor as very dear,
For you are (or will be) each a Queen crowned in Heaven
>   with the Virgin Mary.

— Raphael Brown

II

LETTER OF ST. FRANCIS TO THE BROTHERS AND SISTERS OF PENANCE

An hitherto unknown letter which was written (dictated) by St. Francis to the members of his Third Order, the Brothers and Sisters of Penance, has been found. The original is Manuscript 225 in the Guarnacci Library at Volterra, Italy. Paul Sabatier published the Latin text already in 1900 under the title "Verba vitae et salutis" (Words of life and salvation). However, it was the well known Franciscan scholar, Fr. Cajetan Esser, who recently identified these "Words," on the basis of internal and external criteria, as a letter of St. Francis not previously included among his authentic writings.

That it is a "letter" is evident from the text at the end: "All those into whose hands this letter shall have come." It is quite clearly not an excerpt or abbreviated form of St. Francis' longer Letter to All the Faithful, *which he wrote at a later date and in which he expressed similar ideas. It is an exhortation to "men and women" who "produce worthy fruits of penance," in other words, the Brothers and Sisters of Penance or Tertiaries; and the exhortation is emphasized by a warning about the lot of those "who are not doing penance."*

Could this letter have been the first "rule" or "forma vivendi" (way of life), which St. Francis promised already in 1209 to give to the many married men and women who were so moved by his example and his preaching of penance that they wanted to become his close followers and disciples in a manner similar to that of the Friars Minor? This is not at all impossible.

The very first "rule" that Francis gave to the Friars Minor (his First Order) was very short and simple, consisting mainly of a few gospel texts. His Letter to the Brothers and Sisters of Penance is likewise a short document which points out only some fundamental requirements for a saintly life in the world and, to a great extent, is a mosaic of Scriptural texts. At any rate it is a beautiful and pointed guideline from St. Francis himself for all the men and women in the world who call themselves his spiritual children.

Fr. Cajetan Esser's critical transcript of the original Latin text of this precious document was published in Lettre de Rome *(1977, no. 1, pp. 27-29), which contains a report of a "Congress of the Historians of the Third Order," held in Rome, October, 1976. Soon afterwards it appeared in his new critical edition of the writings of St. Francis:* Die Opuscula des hl. Franziskus von Assisi *(Grottaferrata, Rome, 1976), pp. 176-182. To make the long sentences of the original more readable and understandable, we present our translation in the form of verses and stanzas similar to the method employed in the new Liturgy of the Hours.*

In the Name of the Lord!

Chapter One:
CONCERNING THOSE WHO DO PENANCE

All who love the Lord
  with their whole heart,
  with their whole soul and mind,
  with all their strength,
and love their neighbors as themselves,
and hate their bodies
  with their vices and sins,
and receive the Body and Blood
  of our Lord Jesus Christ,
and produce worthy fruits of penance:

Oh, how happy and blessed
  are these men and women
when they do these things
  and persevere in doing them,
because "the spirit of the Lord
  will rest upon them" (cf. Is. 11:2)
and he will make "his home and dwelling
  among them" (cf. Jn. 14:23),
and they are the sons
  of the heavenly Father (cf. Mt. 5:45),
  whose works they do,
and they are the spouses, brothers,
  and mothers of our Lord Jesus Christ
  (cf. Mt. 12:50).

We are spouses, when by the Holy Spirit
  the faithful soul is united
  with our Lord Jesus Christ.

We are brothers to him, when we fulfill
    "the will of the Father
    who is in heaven" (Mt. 12-50).

We are mothers, when we carry him
    in our heart and body (cf. 1 Cor. 6:20)
    through divine love and
    a pure and sincere conscience;
we give birth to him
    through a holy life
    which must give light to others
    by example (cf. Mt. 5:16).

Oh, how glorious it is to have
    a great and holy Father in Heaven!

Oh, (how glorious it is) to have
    such a beautiful and admirable Spouse,
    the Holy Paraclete!

Oh, (how glorious it is) to have
    such a Brother and such a Son,
    loved, beloved, humble, peaceful,
    sweet, lovable, and desirable above all:
    our Lord Jesus Christ,
    who gave up his life for his sheep
    (cf. Jn. 10:15)
    and prayed to the Father, saying:

"O holy Father,
    protect them with your name
    whom you gave me out of the world.
"I entrusted to them the message
    You entrusted to me,
    and they received it.
"They have known that in truth

I came from you;
   they have believed it was you
   who sent me.
"For these I pray, not for the world.
"Bless and consecrate them, and
   I consecrate myself for their sakes.
"I do not pray for them alone;
   I pray also for those
   who will believe in me
   through their word:
   that they may be holy
   by being one as We are.
"And I desire, Father, to have them
   in my company where I am,
to see this glory of mine
   in your kingdom" (cf. Jn. 17:6-24).

Chapter Two:

CONCERNING THOSE WHO DO NOT DO PENANCE

But all those men and women
   who are not doing penance,
and do not receive the Body and Blood
   of our Lord Jesus Christ,
and live in vices and sins,
and yield to evil concupiscence and
   to the wicked desires of the flesh,
and do not observe

what they have promised to the Lord,
and are the slaves of the world,
    in their bodies, by carnal desires,
    and the anxieties and cares of this life
    (cf. Jn. 8:41):

These are blind, because they do not see
    the true light, our Lord Jesus Christ.
They do not have spiritual wisdom,
    because they do not have the Son of God,
    who is the true Wisdom of the Father.
Concerning them it is said:
    "Their skill was swallowed up"
    (Ps. 107:27), and
    "Cursed are those who turn away
    from your commands" (Ps. 119:21).
They see and acknowledge,
    they know and do bad things
    and knowingly destroy their own souls.

See, you who are blind,
    deceived by your enemies,
    the world, the flesh, and the devil;
for, it is pleasant to the body
    to commit sin
and it is bitter to make it serve God,
because all vices and sins come out
    and "proceed from the heart of man,"
    as the Lord says in the gospel
    (cf. Mk. 7:21).
And you have nothing in this world
    and in the next;
And you thought you would possess
    the vanities of this world
    for a long time.

But you have been deceived;
for the day and the hour will come,
  to which you give no thought
  and which you do not know
  and of which you are ignorant.
The body grows infirm, death approaches,
  and so it dies a bitter death.
And no matter where or when or how
  man dies, in the guilt of sin,
  without penance and satisfaction,
  though he can make satisfaction
  but does not do it:

The devil snatches the soul
  from his body
  with such anguish and tribulation
  that no one can know it
  except he who endures it.
And all the talents and power
  and "knowledge and wisdom"
  (2 Chr. 1:17)
  which they thought they had
  will be taken away from them
  (cf. Lk. 8:18; Mk. 4:25).
And they leave their goods
  to relatives and friends,
  who take and divide them
  and say afterwards:
"Cursed be his soul,
  because he could have given us more,
  he could have acquired more
  than he did."
The worms eat up the body, and so
  they have lost body and soul
  during this short earthly life,

and will go into the inferno
  where they will suffer torture
  without end.

All those into whose hands
  this letter shall have come,
we ask in the charity that is God
  (cf. 1 Jn. 4:16),
to accept kindly and with divine love
  the fragrant words of
  our Lord Jesus Christ,
  quoted above.
And let those who do not know
  how to read have them read to them.

And may they keep them in their mind,
  and carry them out,
  in a holy manner to the end,
  because they are "spirit and life"
  (Jn. 6:64).

And those who will not do this
  will have to render
  "an account on the day of judgment"
  (cf. Mt. 12-36),
  before the tribunal of our Lord
  Jesus Christ (cf. Rom. 14:10).

— *Translated by Marion A. Habig O.F.M.*